The
German
Shorthaired Pointer

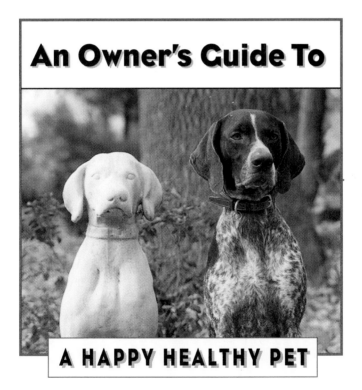

An Owner's Guide To

A HAPPY HEALTHY PET

Howell Book House

Howell Book House
An Imprint of Macmillan General Reference USA
A Pearson Education Macmillan Company
1633 Broadway
New York, NY 10019-6785

Copyright © 1999 by **Howell Book House**
Copyright © all photography by Mary Bloom unless otherwise noted.

Library of Congress Cataloging-in-Publication Data
Campbell, Nancy (Nancy C.)
The German shorthaired pointer : an owner's guide to a happy healthy pet /
Nancy Campbell
  p. cm.
Includes bibliographical references.
ISBN 1-58245-058-7

1. German shorthaired pointer.
SF429.G4C25   1999   99-14625
636.752'5—dc21   CIP

Manufactured in the United States of America
10 9 8 7 6 5 4 3 2 1

Series Director: Amanda Pisani
Book Design: Michele Laseau
Cover Design: Iris Jeromnimon
Illustration: Patricia Douglas
Photography: All photography by Mary Bloom unless otherwise noted.
  Nancy Campbell: 17, 23, 43, 82, 84, 88, 91, 93, 94
  Ann Carter: 38–39
  Howell Book House: 22
  Dr. James Moore: 77
Production Team: Carrie Allen, Oliver Jackson, Clint Lahnen, Christina Van Camp,
  Dennis Sheehan, Terri Sheehan

Contents

part one

Welcome to the World of the German Shorthaired Pointer

1 What Is a German Shorthaired Pointer? 5

2 The German Shorthaired Pointer's Ancestry 17

3 The World According to the German Shorthaired Pointer 26

part two

Living with a German Shorthaired Pointer

4 Bringing Your German Shorthaired Pointer Home 40

5 Feeding Your German Shorthaired Pointer 57

6 Grooming Your German Shorthaired Pointer 66

7 Keeping Your German Shorthaired Pointer Healthy 73

part three

Enjoying Your Dog

8 Basic Training 98
by Ian Dunbar, Ph.D., MRCVS

9 Getting Active with Your Dog 128
by Bardi McLennan

10 Your Dog and Your Family 136
by Bardi McLennan

11 Your Dog and Your Community 144
by Bardi McLennan

part four

Beyond the Basics

12 Recommended Reading 151

13 Resources 155

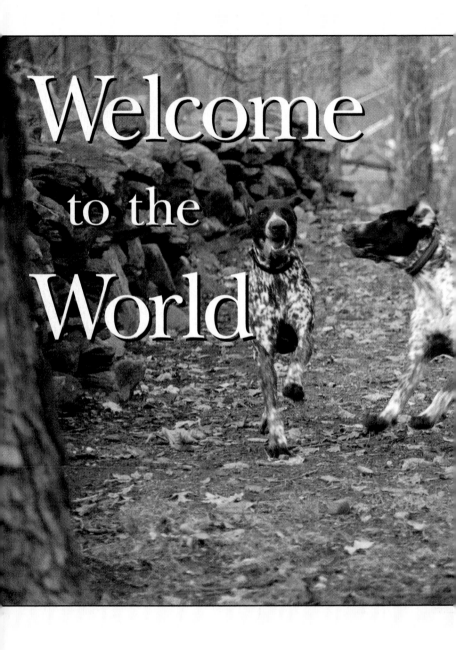

Welcome
to the
World

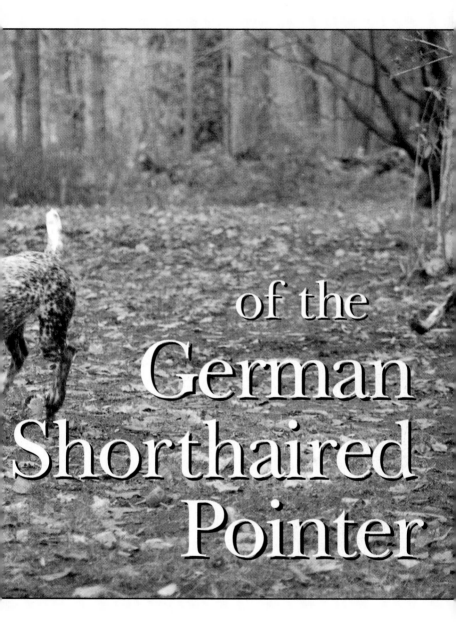

of the
German
Shorthaired
Pointer

External Features of the German Shorthaired Pointer

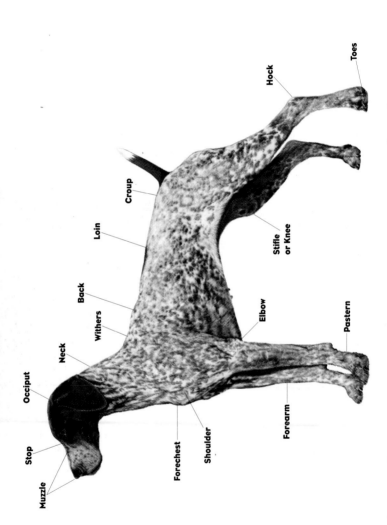

chapter 1

What Is a German Shorthaired Pointer?

"There is no faith which has never yet been broken, except that of a truly faithful dog."
—Konrad Z. Lorenz.

A German Shorthaired Pointer, whether puppy or adult, is a regal comic. It is a close working, multiple purpose hunting dog with boundless energy, love of purpose and dedicated trainability. From the country of origin comes this standard description: ". . . a harmonious dog, whose proportions give a guarantee of endurance, power and speed. Its characteristic features are a noble appearance, graceful outlines, a clean-cut head, a well carried tail and a taut, gleaming coat." In Germany, the Shorthair, as we will call the breed throughout this book, is not only an upland hunter used for finding and pointing birds, but also for trailing furred game and retrieving out of water.

From origins in the nineteenth century until today, however, the Shorthair has found many uses, from hunting birds and other game to tracking, obedience and agility competition, bomb and drug detection and dog sled racing. Shorthairs have been successful assistants to the hearing- and sight-impaired and wheelchair bound, and make cheerful therapy dogs as visitors to hospitals and senior residences.

Whatever the Shorthair trains to do, it does the job with enthusiasm, energy, devotion, dedication and good humor. It is this very energy and positive nature that makes a German Shorthaired Pointer a good choice for an active family willing to devote time and training to a dog. Shorthairs enjoy endless games of ball, fetch and Frisbee with kids or adults, and bond to the family readily. In fact, they do not like to be without their people and are never more joyful than when greeting a homecoming owner.

They make fine running, hiking and biking companions, generally enjoy lifelong good health and most love to ride in the car and swim. Although I have owned many breeds of dogs over the past half century, I have been a devoted German Shorthaired Pointer owner and rescue volunteer for the past twenty-five years. Once you belong to a Shorthair, if it is the right dog for you, you will surely own more than one in your lifetime. I have owned more than a dozen Shorthairs and lived with many a rescue foster dog during the time I have been blessed to know the breed. Each was different, each unique, but each shared the comedic energy of a true German Shorthaired Pointer.

The Breed Standard

The standard for any breed exists to describe characteristics that are the ideal portrayal of a dog that is typical of its breed. To be a good representative of that breed, a dog should have the characteristics outlined in the standard. This is a description that has been developed by the first founders of the breed. These people combined other purebreds over a period of time to get the German Shorthaired Pointer. When they had what they thought looked, acted and worked like the dog they were trying to create, they wrote a breed standard. After a number of generations, the breed is finally considered pure. At various points throughout the history of the breed, the standard may have been modified to refine the description or clarify breed characteristics. This is an ongoing process. The parent club membership of any breed can vote to modify the breed standard periodically.

The parent club of each breed submits the standard to the American Kennel Club (AKC), and the standard becomes the official AKC standard until the national breed club chooses to alter it. It is important to note that the American Kennel Club is only a registry of purebred dogs in this country. The American Kennel Club also creates a forum for conformation and performance

The Shorthair is an aristocratic, well-balanced dog.

events in the United States. Registry with the AKC is not the equivalent of any breed's stamp of approval. Registry with the AKC merely means the dog has, according to the breeder, a father and mother registered as purebred dogs of the same breed with the AKC. Just because a Shorthair is registered with the AKC does not mean it is a good or healthy example of the breed. To get a good dog of any kind, you must first find a good breeder.

You can get a complete copy of the breed standard from the AKC or from the national breed club, and the AKC library can tell you who to call in the parent club for that mailing. If you have Internet access, you can read both the American and international breed standards by going to the GSPCA (German Shorthaired Pointer Club of America) Web site through any Internet search engine.

The overall look of a Shorthair true to type is of an aristocratic, athletic composition with no one part out of

Welcome to the
World of the
German
Shorthaired
Pointer

balance with any other. The dog should look balanced and composed from nose to tail. It is a strong, muscular, active, alert and eager breed, capable of endurance and high performance. It is a hunting dog first, and has an expression of intelligent humor and willingness to please and work for its owner. A Shorthair's high energy should not be mistaken for nervous hyperactivity, and its expression should be of good-natured intensity. Aimless hyperactivity is a fault in any breed.

Once you have read the approved breed standard, you may be able to picture what a good German Shorthaired Pointer looks like, but you will want to visit breeders, conformation shows and field and performance events with this standard in mind to become clearer about variations within the breed. There is quite a lot of difference in size, color and general appearance.

Excerpts from the American Breed Standard follow in italic type: *The overall picture which is created in the observer's eye is that of an aristocratic, well-balanced, symmetrical animal with conformation indicating power, endurance and agility and a look of intelligence and animation. The dog is neither unduly small nor conspicuously large. It gives the impression of medium size, but is like the proper hunter (reference is to a horse hunting with pack hounds) with a short back, but standing over plenty of ground. Tall and leggy dogs, or dogs which are ponderous or unbalanced because of excess substance should be definitely rejected. The first impression is that of a keen enthusiasm for work without indication of nervous or flighty character. Movements are alertly coordinated without wasted motion. Grace of outline, clean-cut head, sloping shoulders, deep chest, powerful back, strong quarters, good bone composition, adequate muscle, well-carried tail and taut coat, all combine to produce a look of nobility and indicate a heritage of purposefully conducted breeding. A judge must excuse a dog from the ring if it displays extreme shyness or viciousness towards its handler or the judge. Aggressiveness or belligerence toward another dog is not to be considered viciousness.*

Faults: Doggy bitches and bitchy dogs are to be faulted.

German, American and international standards all describe the Shorthair as noble looking, having a graceful outline, a tight coat and confident body and tail carriage. These characteristics speak as much about sound temperament as beauty of form. A nervous, shy or hyperactive dog is faulty. A Shorthair can only be powerful if it is well muscled and fit, so a dog that is fat or lacking bone does not fall within the ideals set by the standard.

The Shorthair is of medium size. Males (left) are expected to be slightly taller and heavier than females (right).

Size

Medium size is also prescribed for this breed. The standard actually calls for females in America to be between 21 and 23 inches and 45 to 60 pounds, and males to be between 23 and 25 inches and from 55 to 70 pounds. What this means to me is that a Shorthair should not be as big as a Weimaraner or a Wirehaired Pointer nor as small as a Vizsla—though each of these breeds is also described as medium sized. The German standard calls for slightly taller size limits, and it is noteworthy that many Shorthairs fall outside the standard for size in the U.S. While an inch or more over or under the height standard calls for the judge to penalize the dog if it is being exhibited for conformation, there is no show disqualification for over- or undersize.

The importance of size needs to be considered within the scope of what the owner wants to do with the dog. A large-boned, ponderous dog may not be agile in the

Welcome to the
World of the
German
Shorthaired
Pointer

field and may be a cumbersome companion in a small house. The same dog, however, may be well suited to warding off intruders by its imposing size, particularly if it is also tall.

A small- or fine-boned Shorthair may lack the stamina to work for a long time in field or water but might be a fine companion choice for a smaller home. Regardless of height and substance, no one should have to check the rear end of a Shorthair to tell whether it is a boy or a girl. Females should be feminine and a bit more elegant in appearance and males should have a head somewhat more square and have more bulk to the body.

Head

The head is usually the most distinguishing characteristic of a breed, and that is, to a degree, so of a Shorthair. A Shorthair head should not look like a Labrador Retriever or a Greyhound or a Fox Terrier. It should also not look like more closely related breeds, such as the Weimaraner or the Pointer.

This black and white dog shows the Shorthair's chiseled features.

The German Shorthaired Pointer head should be *clean-cut*. This means that it should have a chiseled appearance, with sculpted looking planes and without excess skin, droopy or rounded elements. The head should be in proportion to the body and look neither like the dog is going to fall over frontward from the weight of its head nor look pinheaded. The skull is broad, slightly rounded and arched on the side. The median indentation between the eyes is not exaggerated, and the bone at the top rear of the skull is not as obvious as it is in the Pointer.

The nose in a liver or brown dog is brown, large, with well open nostrils for better scenting of game. In a black Shorthair, the nose is black. (If the nose is brown, the dog is a liver dog, regardless of how dark the liver color may be. Black pigment in the coat is genetically impossible in a dog with a brown nose.) A spotted or pink nose is faulty. A "flesh-colored" or clear pink nose disqualifies. If you are looking for a pet, however, it is important to remember that some of these faults and disqualifications have only to do with the ideal of breed type and do not impact health, or value as a companion.

The front of the face rises gradually to the forehead with a modest appearance of a transition between nose and brow as a result of the eyebrow position. The top of the muzzle should not have any concave or dish shape or have a definite stop before the brow, as you would see in a proper Pointer.

The muzzle from nose to brow should be the same length to the distance from brow to the top rear of the skull. You will, however, often find Shorthairs who have muzzles shorter than their back skulls. Looking at the head in profile, the muzzle should never appear pointed because of lack of underjaw. Correct muzzle length and formation allow a Shorthair to carry heavy game long distances in the field.

Lips are deep and form a slight fold in the angle of the corner of the mouth. The teeth should form a scissors bite with the front top teeth fitting closely over the bottom teeth. Molars should be present and should mesh, though there is no conformation disqualification for missing teeth.

WHAT YOU SHOULD FIND IN A SHORTHAIR

The German Shorthaired Pointer is a medium-sized, versatile hunting dog with a noble, clean appearance and a confident, good-humored and willing disposition. It is healthy and soundly built with great strength, energy and endurance. A sound dog moves effortlessly with no part interfering with any other. The Shorthair is a square to slightly longer than square dog and gives the impression of balanced proportion with no one part overcoming any other.

When raised with a family, it is a good family companion. It wants to be with its people and learns easily. Structured activity and plenty of exercise are the rule for success.

Hunting is the Shorthair's joy, and this drive can be diverted to other focused activities, which offer exercise and challenge if hunting is not the chosen family sport.

The Shorthair is loyal and bonded to its owner but is able to accept new owners in a remarkably short time if the dog is displaced.

The eyes are almond shape rather than round, and the eyes should neither protrude nor be too deeply set. The skin surrounding the eye should fit well, not turn in toward the eye and irritate the surface, nor hang away from it and collect debris while the dog is running in the field. Eyes ideally should be dark brown and have a lively, sometimes mischievous, but engaging and kind expression. Yellow, blue or white irises are all faulty as they give a startled or staring expression.

The ears help form the Shorthair expression and start just above eye level. They lay flat and are neither too fleshy nor too thin, and they lie close to the head. Proper ear length in an adult allows the ears to reach to the corners of the mouth without being stretched.

The correct Shorthair should have a somewhat square look with a tail that sits high and firm.

Body

The correct Shorthair neck is long enough to allow the dog to reach game on the ground easily. It slopes gracefully from the base of the head to shoulder *on beautifully curving lines* and is muscular and larger at the shoulders. The shoulders are sloping and well muscled. If the shoulders lay on the body where they should, the neck will appear longer and more graceful. If the front leg and shoulder assembly is too far forward on the backbone, the neck will appear short, and the back may appear long.

A moderate throatiness, or excess skin under the neck, is allowed, but the skin is tight overall. The chest should be deeper than broad, reaching down to the elbow of the front leg. Several inches behind the elbow, giving enough room for the front legs to move freely, the ribs expand, or spring out. This gives room for heart and lung function during exercise. The back ribs reach well down just prior to the tuck up of the belly under the loin.

The back appears short, and the dog should look square or slightly longer than square. The tail sits high and firm—it is cut to 40 percent of its length at about 3 days of age. It will sometimes curve slightly, particularly if the dog is excited, but it should not have an exaggerated curve over the back toward the head. The back is firm, and not overly long, swayed or arched more than very slightly over the loin. A steep drop from the hips to the tail origin is faulty. The correct balance in every element of the dog's build allows it to function as intended—as an athletic hunter. Correct and sound structure also promotes soundness and better health and joint function later in life.

Legs viewed from the front appear parallel. The Shorthair's shock absorbers are really the section of the front foot, which looks to be part of the leg. This area is called the pastern and extends from the rear pad, which does not touch the ground, to the toes and footpads, which do. The pastern section should be nearly vertical and provide spring to withstand the stress of hard exercise. The feet should be compact, well arched in the toes with heavy nails and thick, hard pads to withstand the battering of running long distances on rough terrain.

Rear

The hips are broad with sockets wide apart and fall slightly toward the tail in a graceful curve. The thighs have great strength from good muscling. The knee

Welcome to the
World of the
German
Shorthaired
Pointer

joint or stifle is well bent, as is the joint of the hock.
This combination of angles gives drive and traction.
The hocks, seen from the rear, should not point
toward or away from one another, but the lower legs
should stand parallel. Endurance, strength, flexibility,
speed and agility all depend on a sound rear.

*Seen from the
rear, the dog's legs
should appear
parallel (left).*

*Strength and
endurance will be
impeded by a
hocky rear (right).*

Coat

Though the Shorthair coat is softer on the ears and
head and longer on the underside of the tail and back
of the haunches, the body coat should be dense, hard
to the touch and short. Long body hair is a fault, as is
a soft body coat. The harsh coat helps the dog withstand injury while hunting in thick and thorny under-
growth. The coat color can be any combination of liver
and white, solid liver, liver and white ticked, patched or
roan. The American standard calls for any areas of
lemon, orange or black to disqualify in the conformation ring.

Black and black and white Shorthairs are accepted in
the German and international standards, however, and
may be registered with the AKC in this country. They
may participate in all areas of field competition, obedience and other performance events but not the show
ring. Some members of the parent club are working

toward getting the black and black and white coloration accepted in this country as well. Black is a simple dominant gene in the German Shorthaired Pointer and, therefore, cannot appear unless at least one parent of a litter is black. A liver or liver and white Shorthair bred to another of the same color can never produce a black puppy. Regardless of liver or black color, the pup is a Shorthair if its parents are registered Shorthairs. Many breeders think the black and white coloration, which is often accompanied by very dark nose pigment and deep brown eyes, darkens overall pigment in liver offspring. Others say that the black coat color does not bleach out in the sun. People hold strong opinions on the issue of coat color in this breed, so prepare to form your own. It is a question of preference.

Black and white Shorthairs may be registered with the American Kennel Club, but this coloration is currently unacceptable in the show ring.

Movement

Very little is said of correct movement in most sporting dog standards. It is my opinion that movement is one of the most important indicators of how well a dog is built, its endurance in any performance or competition activity and how long it will remain sound into old age. At a trot, the Shorthair gait should be smooth. As speed increases, the legs converge more closely beneath. The standard says that the tendency to single track (to have all the footprints fall in a single line) is

15

Welcome to the
World of the
German
Shorthaired
Pointer

desirable, but this movement should be distinguished from the front legs crossing over the path of one another, or the rear legs brushing or moving too close. These are both movement faults.

A Shorthair should move with little effort and with considerable grace at the trot without rear legs reaching inside, outside or striking the front at the trot, and without the front legs lifting too high and breaking at the pastern (called a hackneyed gait) to avoid the rear legs. Watching the dog move away or toward the viewer, the set of legs farthest away should barely appear behind those nearest in a sound dog. From the side, the dog should seem to move with little effort, with forelegs reaching well ahead as if to pull the dog forward, and the rear driving smoothly with great power. The movement should be so effortless at the trot that the dog seems to float along.

The Bottom Line

It is important to remember that a good breeder will want to breed the best litter it is possible to breed. He or she will breed carefully, with health clearances and attention to sound temperament and hunting talent. It is likely that the breeder will keep the pup best suited to his or her purposes. If you are looking at the standard as a guideline and your goal is to find a handsome, healthy puppy to love or watch in the field, it is more important that your pup have the temperament to fit your lifestyle than conformation that exactly fits the standard. The standard is a guide toward selecting a Shorthair that seems like most good Shorthairs. Small deviations from the standard are acceptable in a pet puppy or adopted companion.

chapter 2

The German Shorthaired Pointer's Ancestry

"A dog is a smile and a wagging tail. What's in between doesn't matter much."
—Clara Ortega

There was a long time before the large estates of Europe broke up, fencing of these great landholdings began and before the use of the double-barreled flintlock to bring down game birds began in the mid-eighteenth cen-

tury. Once, only the royal and the wealthy had access to open land, and only they could afford the packs of dogs needed to hunt a wide variety of game.

Before this time, men and their dogs stalked or drove their prey into traps of various sorts, and game birds were cornered and captured by

Welcome to the
World of the
German
Shorthaired
Pointer

net. A good game bird dog "stood before" or in front of a group of birds on the ground, while hunters netted them from the opposite direction. How things changed when guns, smaller tracts of private land and fencing arrived along with the growth of a more affluent middle class.

Most middle-class German hunters in the nineteenth century wanted a medium-sized hunting dog that would not take up too much room and would manage easily. Because a hunter could afford only one or two dogs, the new dog must search out and find every kind of game, from bird to hare to boar, point them and hold them, be steady to the shot, find and dispatch any wounded game and be a sure retriever from land or water, regardless of hot or cold scent.

This was a new sort of hunter who hunted on occasion, and sometimes for sport. At the end of the hunt, or on days when there was no hunting to do, the same dog should serve to alert the family to the arrival of strangers, and give them the company of a good and loyal companion. Like most dog owners today, this new breed of hunter also wanted his new best friend to be a handsome possession to inspire pride. It was time for a new breed of dog in Germany.

The Development of the Shorthair in Germany

When a community of people develops a new dog breed, it chooses existing breeds and combines them until it produces the dog desired. Then, after many generations, the breeders close the studbooks and declare the breed by name as a "pure" breed. The German Shorthaired Pointer, according to a number of early breed histories, is a combination of several recognized earlier breeds. All of the exact breeds used remain unproven, sometimes contradicted and perhaps even subject to mistranslation.

Many say one breed to make up the old German Pointer is an early "net" dog, the Spanish Pointer, with a fine nose, a skill at holding birds before the net, but too slow and plodding. Some include the "Bloodhound" in the German Shorthaired Pointer heritage—but all agree that this is not the Bloodhound famous for hunting down wanted prisoners on TV. Directly translated, the *"Schweisshund"* means any dog *(hund)* that scents *"schweiss"*—meaning scent, sweat or moisture.

German Pointers of the early 1800s, such as these dogs, exhibited a more coarse, houndlike appearance than the Shorthair of today.

Pictures of some of the very first unregistered German Shorthaired Pointers do, however, resemble the heavy, loose-skinned breed known best for gentle spirit, love of water, great noses, tracking ability and a "soft" retrieving mouth.

There are also some writers who contend that the French were more advanced than the Germans in developing good-looking, well-balanced hunters in the nineteenth century. The thought that French Pointers and Setters influenced the breed we now know as the German Shorthaired Pointer is supported by the fact that the Germans once commanded their pointing dogs in French—which may have indicated that some of the dogs were either bred or trained in France.

The first efforts at developing a breed for the new middle class were localized and informal. A farmer or merchant with a dog that fit the needs of the new breed of

19

Welcome to the
World of the
German
Shorthaired
Pointer

hunter found a fellow hunter with a breeding prospect with the same or better skills, and the development of the breed proceeded. Modest means, communications and travel opportunity kept the breeding opportunities local and limited.

Toward the last quarter of the nineteenth century, however, travel, communications and affluence all increased. It was actually a real prince, by the name of Albrecht Zu Solms-Bronfels, who inspired the notion of looking to the dog's function to create a standard for the breed. His own dog, Feldman I, was neither noble in appearance nor elegant, but the prince liked the way it hunted, and it was faster than the original German Pointer.

THE SHORTHAIR BECOMES "OFFICIAL"

The first registry of pedigrees for German Shorthaired Pointers formed in 1872, and the first of the "breed" ever to be registered was a dog named Hector I, who was a far more handsome dog than Prince Solms's unregistered Feldman I. The prince started a school in his region with methods of testing both conformation and hunting ability.

In 1877, the first dog show with classes for the Shorthair took place in Vienna, Austria, and the first breed standard was approved by 1889.

Dr. Paul Kleeman, whose devotion to the Shorthair was a direct result of working with the prince, became the first president of a brand-new breed club for Shorthairs. It was called the Klub Kurzhaar—simply, The Shorthair Club. Hunting tests, called Derbies, started in 1893 and were held in the spring. The Utility Search tests held in the fall tested both natural and learned skills. The Utility Search test

---

FAMOUS OWNERS OF GERMAN SHORTHAIRED POINTERS

Roy Rogers and Dale Evans

Bo Derek

Andy Williams

Harry Connick Jr.

Julio Iglesias

Clark Gable

Ben Stein

Robert Urich

Clarence Gaines

Christy Turlington

---

was named the Solms Memorial in 1903, in honor of the Prince of Shorthairs. The event is now referred to as the Kleeman-Solms (KS), and dogs that qualify must have both worthy field skills and meet the conformation standard. If they pass, they receive a title of Seiger. You will find this KS title in pedigrees of American dogs with ancestors that have passed the rigorous German test.

Non-German Influences

The German Shorthaired Pointer was also influenced by events outside of Germany. The first Field Trial for Pointers and Setters took place in Staffordshire, England, in 1866. The first one in America, also for Pointers and Setters, occurred in 1874 in Tennessee. So, long before the full development of the German Shorthaired Pointer, field competition was informing the breed's founders.

In 1907, a black Arkwright Pointer, named Beechgrove Bess, was imported to Germany by the merchant Christian Bode. Bode had traveled in England on business and liked the fieldwork of the best of the Pointers. He wanted to be sure German Shorthaired Pointers were at least their equal. He introduced Bess to his breeding program, some say to add darker pigment in coat, eyes and nose, and a higher held head for when scenting conditions required it. The majority of authorities agree that the most significant contribution of Pointer blood was greater speed and a higher held head while scenting game.

The Breed Is Fine-Tuned

The early part of the twentieth century saw the breed strengthen desirable characteristics and eliminate dogs too extreme in one feature or another, with light eyes or too much or too little bone, less than desirable hunting style or faulty temperament. It was a time for focus and improvement.

Shorthairs in America

Early in 1925, Dr. C. R. Thornton from Montana saw an article on German Shorthairs in a magazine entitled

Welcome to the
World of the
German
Shorthaired
Pointer

the *National Sportsman*. Shortly after, he had contacted a breeder in Austria, and imported the first recorded example of the breed in America. Its name was Senta V. Hohenbruch. When you read Thornton's description of his beloved first Shorthair, it seems the dog was the epitome of determination, skill, kindness and intelligence. The American love of this breed of "every use" had begun, and it still continues.

While many fine breeders have contributed to the caliber and enduring quality of the breed in this country and others over time, this book is too small a space to offer them homage. Other books have done this job well, and some are included in the bibliography. If a person wants to learn more about specific dogs in a pedigree, deeper research is required. A fortunate novice will have the good luck to be taken under the wing of someone advanced, experienced and a champion of breed history.

The first recorded Shorthair in America was Senta v. Hohenbruch, imported by Dr. Charles R. Thornton.

I was lucky to have Charles Gandal, DVM, as a horse veterinarian and friend as I began my quarter-century journey with the German Shorthaired Pointer. It was the breed's kindness and generosity of spirit that directed me to Ken and Judy Marden of Crossing Creek German Shorthaired Pointers. Ken was then president of the American Kennel Club, and Judy a wellspring of breed knowledge and history. They were and are firm believers in the breed's versatility—that Shorthairs can and should succeed at every task they are set to—from hunting to performance events to hospital visits. From my beginnings in showing to hunting advice and even to rescue, I owe endless thanks to these three for pushing me toward the breed at first, and further into it with each new generation. Those now in the breed, and the breed itself, owe these people, and too many others to mention, a bow of gratitude.

Today's Shorthairs are versatile hunting dogs—this breed champion was painted by the author.

The breed continues today, for the most part, as versatile hunting dogs and household companions. To quote the man who first brought his beloved Senta to America back in 1925, "They are essentially a family or one man dog. Good disposition, Love to be caressed. Take kindly to children, and show almost human intelligence in looking after small tots. As companions and pals, they are next to man. As hunting dogs they will hunt anything from duck to deer. Primarily, they are bird dogs; but I have never attempted hunting anything from mouse to moose, that they were not ready and willing to assist."

The Shorthair Today

Unlike many breeds, the German Shorthaired Pointer has remained, for the most part, a unified breed. If you want a dog for casual upland game hunting, the Shorthair can still do the job.

If you are determined to compete in Field Trials, the Shorthair is a thrilling partner in a competitive field. One thing can be said without question, the Shorthair has the heart, the will and the stamina for serving its owner in field competition. If you have a softer intention, but still like to socialize with your Shorthair while letting it enjoy the work it was bred to do, The American Kennel Club Hunt Tests may be for you. They fall into three categories, Junior, Senior and Master levels. The Junior level tests natural ability at pointing, finding game and trainability. The Senior level demands more solid hunting skills, both natural and trained, and the Master level tests a finished gun dog. You may want to contact the American Kennel Club for information on Field Trials and Hunting Tests to see if either, or even both, are of interest to you.

Many show dogs compete regularly in hunting tests, and the pride of the breed is still the dual champion—the Shorthair that has completed both a conformation championship and a field championship. To do so, however, requires a great deal of time, training and travel. There are many dogs who likely could achieve the dual, but whose owners have neither the means, the time nor the inclination to compete for championship titles. Many will choose one area of activity that is a happy occupation for themselves and their dog.

Many show champions are also successful field competitors.

The greatest number of Shorthairs are doubtless in the homes of two categories of owner: the companion household, where the sole goal is to have a handsome, personable pet, and the home of the occasional bird hunter. Often, these houses are the same one!

More recently, Shorthairs have found work in police departments, particularly in drug detection and search and rescue. The ability of a Shorthair to scent a desired objective is part of what makes it such a good hunting companion. As numbers of Shorthairs have been successful in tracking tests, it is a natural next step to search and rescue and substance detection. One of the main characteristics that makes a Shorthair a likely choice for such work is its natural determination and intensity.

Today, most breeders encourage their new puppy owners to find structured work for their Shorthairs to do when the owners have the time to spend with them and give them the attention they deserve and need. Once they are full-grown, Shorthairs are ideal companions for both fitness and distance runners. They have stamina, and they always want to go with you, regardless of what the destination or activity might be. Shorthairs even enjoy flyball competition with other dogs and teams, and have a great time posing for advertising photography and stealing the stage wherever they go. It is hard to avoid a Shorthair.

Whatever the use a Shorthair may be put to, when it passes on, it will be rightly buried in the heart of its owner. Once a Shorthair has taken possession of your life, it is likely it will do what the breed has done since its early German origin—take possession of your being. That part of Shorthair breed history never changes.

The athletic Short-hair is a natural at agility trials.

chapter 3

The World According to the **German** **Shorthaired** **Pointer**

"Puppies are nature's remedy for feeling unloved . . . plus numerous other ailments of life."—Richard Allen Palm

The Proper Fit

When people call me looking for a puppy or a rescue dog, they generally want to know if I have a dog for them. This is normal. Nonetheless, it is more useful for me to ask, "Are you right for a German Shorthaired Pointer?"

Here is one dog's description of the right kind of person for a Shorthair: "My person should have lots of energy, and like to hike, run, swim and play ball sports. My person should have tons of time to keep me company, a big fenced yard where we can both play and my human should not be too fussy about things in general. My human should be fairly smart, or I may outwit him or her, just for fun. My human need not be a hunter, but he or she should not mind that hunting is part of who I am, and my hunting energy will have to be absorbed in other challenges, if hunting is not the game of choice. My human should understand and be tolerant of enthusiasm and not be impatient with unbridled joy, even if it is inconvenient at the time. Most importantly, my human must have a sense of humor, be willing to share almost everything—and be forgiving."

Many people screening for proper owners for other sporting dogs, the Labrador Retriever, for example, say it is not the right dog for everyone. That statement can be doubled, even squared, for the Shorthair.

YOUR LIFESTYLE

If you are laid back, quiet, sedentary, the indoor type and would rather drive than walk even short distances, a Shorthair may overwhelm you. If you are a person who is about to commit to a change from sedentary to athletic for the sake of your heart, mind or psyche, however, a Shorthair in your home may be just the right daily stimulus, and friend. A Shorthair is a whirlwind of athletic energy, a demanding play partner, an insistent companion and a comically annoying amusement. To be happy with your Shorthair, you need time and energy, and you need to regard caring for a dog as your bond and your joy. A Shorthair will not be neglected. When in the yard, she will want you to witness her squirrel finds and chipmunk sightings, if at all possible. If you are gardening, she will often "help" you dig, or drop a tennis ball in the middle of your newly raked leaves, as if to say "Enough of this make-work tidiness; let's get on to something more important, like ball!"

CHARACTERISTICS OF A GERMAN SHORTHAIRED POINTER

Comical

Noble

Energetic

Athletic

Owner bonded

Intelligent

Needs exercise and structured play

Quick learner

Needs fencing

Needs a devoted owner

Welcome to the
World of the
German
Shorthaired
Pointer

When you bathe and brush up in the morning, you may find your Shorthair under your feet, begging for her share of the hot air from the blow-dryer or eyeing the bar of soap or the toothpaste tube greedily. More than once have I found myself "joined" in my shower by my fondest Shorthair.

If you confine a Shorthair away from you, you may find her sitting and sighing or whining outside the door when you emerge. Then, she will bounce to her feet, toy in mouth, ready to resume real life—with you! A Shorthair will succeed in a home where the dog is planned as an equal family member—where her needs are considered by all to be just as vital as those of Mom or Dad or the kids.

THE TYPICAL SHORTHAIR MORNING

You would like to awaken at six or seven, but your Shorthair knows that dawn is the correct time to wake up. She will climb on the bed, stick her cold, wet nose under your arm or simply sit over you, staring down her nose at you, until the discomfort of being watched intently overwhelms you and you stumble to your feet. Alternately, she may stuff dirty socks in your face, or sit next to the bed holding one of your shoes. If you become irritated by this intrusion, she may bounce eagerly on the bed and begin to wash your lips, nose and eyelids—just to get the day off to a clean start. Regardless of method, your Shorthair is in charge of waking you. She takes her job seriously, and now you are awake and cannot return to sleep.

I'm up! Let me out!

Let Me Out!

By this time, the Shorthair is twirling in front of you toward the door, bounding intermittently, sometimes emitting strange sounds of Shorthair glee. It is, after all, morning. The beginning of all things to be eaten, chased, alerted, dug up and fetched. No better time to celebrate!

Now Let Me In!

Once the morning constitutional is complete, food must follow immediately. The dog will show you where her food is kept—every day—as though you were suffering amnesia. She will follow you every step of the way in food preparation, sitting several times to let you know she is quite ready to eat. Owners who have properly taught their dog who is the boss will make the dog sit and wait to eat. While this is going on, your Shorthair will either stomp her front feet, whine or look sad. You will give up and offer the meal faster than you had planned. Then she will finish off her grub so fast you feel guilty for giving her so little. Do not be fooled. This is merely a Shorthair trick. Do not feed her more than she needs regardless of this emotional blackmail. A fat Shorthair will be the result. It is not a pretty sight.

Now it is your turn to eat . . . while you would like to sit and have coffee and a nibble for yourself, your Shorthair will either sit directly in front of you drooling like a deer on opium, and seeming malnourished, or she will try and distract you, getting you to leave your food unattended so she can grab it while you are not looking. If you are a trained human, you will have learned how to command, "Go to your place," and, "Down/stay." If you decide to do this, be prepared for deep, sad, longing looks and heavy sighing. Alternately, she will want you to go back out with her, so finally, you dutifully carry your morning ration outside where you will begin to fetch the odd object and enjoy a bracing dawn of walking, dizzy discovery and laughter. She is teaching you the joy of morning—even in rain or snow.

If you attempt self-defense and close your dog outside, she is only good for about as long as it takes her to chase a single sparrow or corner the cat. She will be back at the door, sitting, perhaps whining for a visit from her

Welcome to the
World of the
German
Shorthaired
Pointer

Dog GOD. That would be you. Dog GOD is a serious responsibility, and it is a mantle every Shorthair owner must put on. Worship for a Shorthair is a way of life.

As you ready yourself for the day, you will have either a witness or a participant. Shorthairs are not the breed for people who find solace in being alone. Shorthairs do not agree with this mode of living. They are pack animals, and you, for one, are their pack. If you get another dog, preferably a Shorthair to keep your first one company, then you will have two at your heels at all times. It will feel like you are being followed by a school of fish. They want you with them. It is love.

You are the most important member of your Shorthair's pack, and your dog wants to spend time with you (the author with Mikey).

Shorthairs do not like to remain behind quietly while their pack leader works an eight-, ten- or twelve-hour day. This is not negotiable. To start off a puppy in this fashion is inviting household and psychological disaster. The pup cannot learn how to be a sane and cooperative family member if left alone. Think about it. She will be lonely, bored, have lots of unused energy to motivate her and there will be no authority figure there to teach her how to grow up. What you cannot expect of a human child, you cannot expect of a Shorthair baby. At each end of the day, and preferably in the middle, should be some serious structured but off-leash exercise. Simple walking is not enough for a Shorthair, so getting a dog walker, while better than nothing, is not sufficient to use up your dog's ample energy. If you live near a family with responsible junior high or high school children, hiring a child whose family cannot have a dog to play Frisbee within a fenced enclosure can lead to a happy Shorthair (and a happy neighbor child). If there is a runner in your neighborhood who works at home and likes to take a midday break, perhaps you can encourage him or her to take your dog along. Your Shorthair will be more civilized when you get home.

Training for Shorthairs

Although good training is essential for sensible life with any dog, multiply the need for training with a Shorthair. Respect is essential in the relationship, and it goes both ways, but basic training (see chapter 8) is a must whether you buy a puppy or adopt an older dog. Proper training gives a Shorthair security, bonds her to the trainer and allows civilized life to go forward tolerably. It is an investment in time, but most kennel clubs hold an obedience class one night a week for six to eight weeks duration, and that is a good way to start.

Some owners choose a trainer to take the dog away and train her, then return to give a small lesson in technique to the owner. This works for some breeds, but is not recommended for a Shorthair. Bonding and mutual respect are the reason it is better to develop your own training skills and train the dog yourself. If you prefer to have a professional come in, be sure he or she is training you, and you are training the dog. Training goes on for the life of your Shorthair. You must enforce the work learned, daily at first, and then periodically thereafter to ensure a sound relationship, lifelong. Be sure to ask for references from any training professional. Remember that obedience trainers and behavioral trainers need not be licensed, and there are very few educational routes around the country for people wishing to learn how to become professional trainers. Shorthairs can be a handful, but they are surprisingly prone to suffer from inappropriate or hard-handed training techniques. Choose your training atmosphere and your trainer carefully.

Welcome to the
World of the
German
Shorthaired
Pointer

A Shorthair is an odd combination of sensitivity and will-fulness. Corporal punishment is not recommended—not even for the worst of sins. The best way to get your Shorthair to get it right is to distract her from the unwanted behavior, replace the unwanted behavior with a desirable, learned behavior and enforce the new behavior. Yelling only tells your Shorthair one of two things: A) You are lonely, or B) You are frightened. Neither thing tells the Shorthair to change her be-havior. Yelling just makes everyone unhappy and nervous.

By training your dog, you develop the bond between you.

In general, Shorthairs are pushy, so teaching yours to sit at the door and wait while you exit first is a good practice. Waiting for food delivery until you give permission is also rec-ommended. Asking a Shorthair to do something to get what she wants, even petting and stroking, leads to a dog that works for her owner, instead of an owner that is com-manded by his or her dog. Try to "insee" your dog clearly, and your training will go more smoothly. Re-member that a Shorthair is not like a Collie or a Borzoi, and must be trained differently. A training formula that will work for a herding dog will not work for a sporting dog, and a training protocol that will work for a Labrador Retriever will not work for a Shorthair. And, of course, every Shorthair is different.

The Sensitive Shorthair

The Shorthair will give back to her owner whether asked to or not. On those days when I have been ill and confined in bed, I will drearily waken to find one or two of my own Shorthairs flanking my sides, keeping me warm, eyeing me sadly with worried sighs and solemn, soft brown eyes, inspecting me queru-lously. Others may have taken up the door or the rug at the foot of the bed to guard my sleep and make me well. This is a day when there will be no rousting out of my bed, no busy footsteps in the hall and no twirling toward the door. They have softly gone about their needed morning outing with my husband, and they are back. They are very, very quiet. Shorthairs worry, you know.

You've Made the Decision

If my description of a morning in the life of a Shorthair has not put you off and you are ready to know more, it is time to coach you about how to choose the right Shorthair for you, bring her into your life successfully and become a Shorthair fanatic.

Structured playtime is critical to a Shorthair's well-being.

VERIFY YOUR MOTIVES AND ABILITIES

Remember these several things about life with a Shorthair:

- you are the center of her world
- training is not just desirable, it is a mandate
- the dog's energy must be consumed by structured play
- you must supervise when young children are around (this is true with any dog but more so with one that twirls and bounces)
- in most cases, confinement when you are away is essential until the dog is well beyond 2 years of age
- use a firm but jolly voice and a confident hand

33

Welcome to the
World of the
German
Shorthaired
Pointer

- do not baby a Shorthair or you will have a 60- or 70-pound brat

- use your wits—your Shorthair may be the smartest being you currently know

When determining if you are Shorthair ready, the most important questions are about yourself, once you have learned enough about the breed. If you have any doubts, review your decision. Shorthairs are not for everyone. They are unique, natural antidepressants and wonderful and loving companions. They are not, however, easy to put on automatic pilot. Be sure you are ready for such a commitment before you buy or adopt.

OTHER PETS AND SHORTHAIRS

Dogs

Shorthairs like to be with other dogs, if they have been raised with other dogs, and they are eager playmates with their own kind. They are, however, prey-driven, and a small, fluffy toy dog may resemble some other kind of prey to them. If they have been raised with small dogs, or are mild-mannered by nature, they may have a fond and lifelong friendship with a small friend. Introducing an adult Shorthair who has been avidly hunted to a small dog may lead to disaster. Go carefully.

If you have a cat at home and plan to adopt an adult dog, look for a dog that has a good history with feline companions.

Cats

All of our dogs have grown up with our rescue Siamese, and they regard him as one of the pack. Many mornings I am amused to see the five big dogs gamboling out into the woods with the Siamese following along behind as though he is one of them. He will swat playfully at the dogs when they get too pushy, and run wildly around to entice them. The worst experience he has ever suffered from them is a wet fur mouth bath. As he is not afraid of the dogs, however, he was not prepared for one of our rescues who was a confirmed cat killer. I was fast enough to extricate the cat from this ill-intentioned older Shorthair, but had I not been there and alert, the cat would not have been gently retrieved to hand. If you have a cat and are adopting a Shorthair, make sure the dog is cat-safe before you commit.

Birds

Birds are another story. These dogs are natural bird dogs, and some are more intent at it than others. Because Shorthairs are quite intelligent and discriminating in general, they will learn which prey you want them to hunt in the field, and learn you "don't want" field mice, for example. This same "leave it" command can be exercised with caged birds in the home, especially if the dog has been in the presence of the caged bird since puppyhood. You need not worry about the dog leaping on the cage and toppling it to extricate the bird inside. Would I leave a bird loose in the house with a Shorthair? No more than I would leave a fox loose in a hen house.

Small Pets

You must take care if you have guinea pigs, gerbils, hamsters, white mice, rabbits or other small creatures, including pet snakes. Shorthairs hate snakes in general, and will grab them up and shake them to death unless they have been effectively snake-proofed for hunting. Use common sense and do not presume anything. It will prevent unwanted disaster.

Household Items and Furniture

Any large dog will have some impact on the household. A Shorthair is not an exception, and her verve and bounding enthusiasm may change your household in ways that you had not considered. Low tables with delicate objects may have to be changed to tall shelves with delicate objects. Fringed tablecloths can be tantalizing for a puppy or adolescent Shorthair, and garbage that is unprotected is fair game.

Think twice about adding a Shorthair to your life if you insist on spotless white carpets, smudgeless woodwork, food cluttered counter space or dining on the floor in front of the TV.

The Shorthair wants to share everything from sandwich to sofa. Although some obedience and behavioral training can limit the most extreme of these tendencies, it is the nature of the Shorthair to nuzzle, lap sit, await her share of your edibles, find great treats left behind by the lazy folks who do not put food away and occupy the most esteemed seat in the house.

Many times on arriving in the living room, hands full of snacks, we find that the Shorthairs have occupied every sitting surface. Of course, we have more of these wonderful creatures than anyone should, but even one can occupy an entire mega sofa. When you ask them to move to their own bed, they have become deaf, paralytic and so suddenly heavy and stiff as to be unmovable.

You can teach your Shorthair the house rules with no problem—if you apply the rules consistently.

SETTING LIMITS IN THE HOME

We decided long ago to live mutual life with our Shorthairs, but that may not be comfortable for everyone, such as your mother-in-law or business guests. If you are going to set limits some of the time, start early and set limits all of the time. Do not ask the Shorthair to snuggle with you on the sofa during a thunderstorm and a monster movie because you need the company and then banish her to the floor when whim dictates.

Start sending your dog to her own place when she is young and occasionally join her there. Shorthairs love nothing better than your furniture, unless that might be your lap. At 60 or 70 pounds, some owners find themselves overwhelmed as the cute puppy achieves full scale in only a few months. Have a family conference and decide what everyone wants to do. If one of the children wants the dog to sleep in his or her very own bed, the dog is fully able to learn that a single bed in the house is free game, but all others are off-limits. This is true of a special chair or sofa. The Shorthair can learn most things she needs to know. It is usually the humans who spoil things by being inconsistent and changing their minds.

More Information on the Shorthair

NATIONAL BREED CLUB

The German Shorthaired Pointer Club of America
4103 Walnut St.
Shaw AFB, SC 29152-1429
(803) 499-4140

You may also call the club secretary for the contact information for a local club in your area.

BOOKS

Byrne, Georgina. *The German Shorthaired Pointer.* O'Connor, Western Australia: Austed Publishing Co., 1990.

McKowen, Robert H. *The New Complete German Shorthaired Pointer.* New York: Howell Book House, 1998.

Sutsos, Mike and Robert Lee Behme. *Training Your Pointer and Spaniel.* New York: G. P. Putnam's Sons, 1987.

MAGAZINES

GSP News

Monthly magazine devoted to the Shorthair. Call the editor at: (518) 761-6763 for subscription information, or e-mail: GSPNEWS2@aol.com.

BREEDER REFERRAL

(315) 626-2990

REFERENCES

The American Kennel Club: (212) 696-8200 or http://www.akc.org

RESCUE INFORMATION AND ADOPTIONS

(520) 476-3779
or to adopt: http://www.gsprescue.org

Living
with a

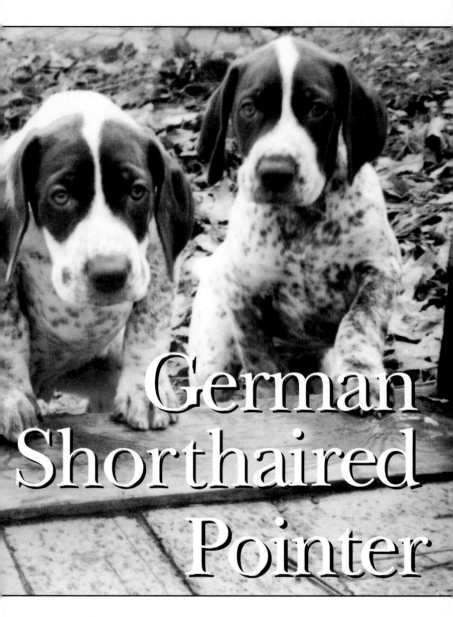

part two

German Shorthaired Pointer

Bringing Your
German Shorthaired
Pointer
Home

Choosing the
Right Dog for You

*"No one appreciates the very special
genius of your conversation as a
dog does."* —Christopher Morley

Tradition, childhood memories
and Madison Avenue have all
taught you that your adult life
is due a modest sense of well-
being, a family and a family dog
that starts as a puppy—usually
on Christmas or a birthday. Maybe not.

First, never get anything alive for
anyone who is not a participant
in the decision. Second, do not give puppies for Christmas or any
other day of celebration. Cast off Christmas Shorthair gift puppies

keep German Shorthair Pointer Rescue busy through-out spring and summer. Just say no to Santa.

If all have agreed that this Christmas purchase is to be a puppy, put a picture of the intended pup in a box to open and wait until after the hazards and hullabaloo of Christmas are over to go pick up the pup. If children are involved, a stuffed puppy toy will fill in the gap. When you do go get your new family member, it will make those dark days between Christmas and the New Year very bright indeed. Anticipation sweetens discovery.

While most people think that buying a puppy is the only way to get a dog, that thinking is no longer totally valid. You need to ask yourself what you know about raising a puppy. Maybe the last time a puppy was a part of your life, it was merely a fond childhood memory—and your mother or father actually raised and trained the pup while you looked on and enjoyed the benefits. A puppy is only a puppy for the course of about three months. By the time a German Shorthaired Pointer is 5 or 6 months old, he may weigh between 50 and 70 pounds. He had better be through his basic training by that point, or life as you know it will change. Be sure you are ready for a new canine baby in the house. It is quite a great challenge, and the commitment of time is similar to that of having a new child.

CONSIDER ADOPTING AN ADULT DOG

If you will not be able to spend the time required to raise a puppy, or if you want to try out the breed with the thought of maybe having two a little later, you may want to think of adopting a "kindly used" Shorthair. This is a sensible alternative to sleepless nights and days totally occupied with a dog tot.

Because Shorthairs are a healthy breed, often living more than a dozen lively years, their owner's lives can change radically, long before the dog is old. Rehoming is not uncommon for long-lived breeds. It is definitely not true that the only Shorthairs up for adoption are either aggressive, abused or neglected. Many are of fine breeding, and their families have simply had a life change that will no longer include them. This is often good luck for a person who needs a Shorthair already housetrained, with some obedience and/or hunting training and whose skills and limitations as an adult can be well-known before the adoption decision.

Good Shorthairs may be given up for adoption due to divorce, job change, the passing of an owner, the kids going off to college or the decision to move into a retirement community that does not allow dogs. Today, people wishing to give up their dogs contact rescue organizations in their region for placement help. Your local shelter, veterinarian, Internet search engines or American Kennel Club Library can help you contact a volunteer in your region or provide a referral number from the German Shorthaired Pointer Club near you.

A former rescue dog, Exley has proven himself a wonderful companion.

A rescued dog may not need the same level of training or constant contact as a puppy. Remember that cute bundle of bouncing joy at 8 weeks weighs about 60 pounds as an adolescent only six to eight months later. Puppyhood is very brief, adolescence is seemingly endless and adulthood is the truly enjoyable part of a dog's life—if the correct things are done at the beginning. The good news about Shorthairs is that they rebond, learn new things quickly and are incredibly resilient and flexible in the face of changing owners.

There is more good news about this alternative choice. You can save the life of a worthy dog. Moreover, adopting a dog teaches the children in your family the worth of saving a dog in need, doing a good work and caring for others. If the dog has had a successful life with children previously, he might be an excellent choice for your family.

A Successful Start

Whether an adult or a puppy has been the choice, bring your new family member home when you have time to get to know him, spend time with him, learn about him and let him teach you who he is and what he needs. Do this only when you have the time and want to invest in the process as much as the product. Some people actually charge home with a puppy or dog, put

him in a crate or pen and carry on with a life too busy to enjoy even before the pressure of a new pup. After all, you are getting a Shorthair because it is a breed that wants to keep you company, do things with you and belong to and with you. Take time off, if you need to.

FINDING A PUP

If you have decided that your life and family are best suited to a puppy just now, be prepared to find the most highly reputable breeder you can. If a person's name keeps coming up again and again as you do your research as "the best" and "doesn't approve everyone," locate that person. If you do not know where to start, talk with several veterinarians in your area, and try to get them to refer you to happy Shorthair owners who are clients of theirs and who keep praising and keep in touch with their breeder. Interview them about their ownership experience and who bred their dog.

If a puppy is right for you, find a breeder who is highly regarded.

You may also call the American Kennel Club (AKC) for a breeder in your area, but remember, breeders pay for this referral service, and the AKC does not "recommend" the breeders on their lists. The listing is only an advertising service. You may also go to dog shows and to other performance events and ask people who have dogs whose looks and temperament you like where they got their dog, and if they think the breeder is a good one. Don't jump in and commit to the first "breeder" you meet who is having a litter. He may not be raising the type of Shorthair you need. He may not do health clearances that help ensure a healthy puppy, and he may be somewhat overzealous in telling you just why his pups will be the very best. Get references. Talk to a lot of people. It will pay off in the long run.

Look for an "All-Purpose" Dog

I would try to find a private breeder who shows, is active in obedience or other performance work with his dogs and whose dogs have been successfully hunted as personal gun dogs. I would be hesitant to select a breeder whose interest is strictly field trialing and who also raises dogs only in kennels away from the house. Sometimes such dogs have only been kennel dogs for several generations, and it is unknown whether the line still lives well in the household. Field competition dogs may have been bred for generations to run great distances with endurance and drive, and unless you wish to engage in field trials yourself, one of these dogs may not be for you. If, however, the puppies are related to a calm and companionable field competitor, you may have struck upon a good choice.

Get Ready to Be Grilled . . .

If you meet a breeder you like over the phone, expect the third degree as you tell him of your interest in buying one of his puppies. He will ask you many questions, put a lot of limits on placement and insist on an iron-clad contract agreement. This is a sign of a responsible breeder—one who really cares about the well-being of the pups he brings into the world. Trust your instincts about whether you could relate to this person for the next fourteen years of your Shorthair's life—ask yourself whether he is a person you might like to know regardless of your dog relationship. Think about whether he seems like someone you could interrupt in the middle of a busy weekend and ask a lot of questions about a condition or a behavior that has you worried. If the answer is "yes," ask if he will give you the names of a few of his puppy owners to talk to. Talking to other people who own his dogs will give you more information about how he exercises his contracts and how he has responded to owners' needs.

. . . And to Do Some Grilling

Ask the breeder about the dam of the litter and if you can see her when you come to visit the pups. The dam's personality will have a large influence on that of her puppies. Ask whether the breeder routinely does puppy temperament tests and if sire and dam and a good many dogs behind them in the pedigree have had health clearances before breeding. Hip x-rays and Orthopedic Foundation For Animals (OFA) or Penn Hip hip joint certification, specialist's certifications for eyes and hearts are all standard for today's private Shorthair breeder. Ask what sort of health guarantee he provides, should you discover the puppy has a heritable disorder later. If all goes well, you have the best preparation for bringing your Shorthair home—you have a good breeder.

You want a strong, healthy puppy, so don't hesitate to ask the breeder about the health of the dogs in the puppy's pedigree.

If the breeder you have found, trust and have chosen is not breeding right away, wait for him to do so, or ask him to refer you to another reputable breeder. You will have your puppy for about fourteen years. There is no point in rushing into the wrong situation. Most reputable breeders will also make clear, either verbally or in writing, that they will be there to help for the life of the dog. They do not wish anything they have bred to end up unwanted, in a shelter or worse.

Let Your Breeder Be Your Guide

Presuming you have found the breeder for you, there are still some protocols to observe. "Pick of the litter" is a rather outdated idea. If the breeder wishes to retain some pups for show or competition, and you simply want a companion, the breeder may narrow the choice list for you. If the breeder does standard puppy temperament tests, ask about results and recommendations of which puppy would be right for the home you have described to him. I believe you should not pick a Shorthair because of color, markings or gender.

A good breeder will be able to advise on which puppy in a litter would best suit your lifestyle.

If you are going to get a companion dog but not show him or do advanced level hunting competition or performance events, you will probably be asked to neuter your pet by a specific time. This is commonly stated in your contract.

If you neuter (and if you are getting the dog as a pet only, you should), gender should make no significant difference, as neutering is done earlier than was once the case. Color should not be a deciding factor either, and early coloration may well change. Shorthairs are born white, and the places that will be dark patches later, like the head or any large body patches, are very evident. Unless the pup has a recessive gene combination for bright white background—and there is nothing wrong with such coloration—the little flecks of color, called ticking, will continue to become more and more dense during the first several years of the dog's life. If your choice is a solid liver, of course, the color will be evident at birth, and one of the parents will have had to be solid liver.

Let your breeder be your guide. If you are not going to hunt your Shorthair, for example, then choosing a puppy with less prey drive may be best for you. Responsible breeders are alert to the fit between you and your puppy. They are an invaluable resource.

The Breeder Will Provide

When you go get your puppy, your breeder will probably have supplied you with transitional food and feeding recommendations, puppy supplies and rearing instructions. Do not let well-meaning friends confuse you. Listen to your breeder who raises this breed and knows how to do it successfully. If you have taken the time to find the very best breeder and waited for just the right puppy, you will want to use the help offered. Keep the phone number handy. If you find yourself without a good resource to turn to, be sure to find a good veterinarian and keep this book readily accessible.

Picking Up Puppy

When you go to get your puppy, make sure you take enough time to listen to instructions. Take a collar that will expand with the puppy's first growth spurts, with an ID tag on it. You can order your ID tag just as soon as you know you are getting a pup. Put your phone number on it. (You do not need to wait to know your dog's name. The phone number is enough.) Bring a leash in case the pup needs to relieve himself on the way home. Take your camera and ask the breeder to photograph you with the pup before departure—you will cherish this photograph later. You may even want a photo of the breeder with the pup or the dam. Putting together your Shorthair's photo album through the life of the dog is one of the joys of ownership.

When you plan your journey, it is best to have one person drive and one to hold the puppy. Take two towels for your lap and a plastic bag, as puppies may get carsick on the way home. If it is cold out, warm up the car before departure. Some breeders supply a small swatch of bedding that smells like home—a great idea. Others include puppy's first toys, a stuffed animal and a chew bone. If your breeder does not, make sure you have toys and soft bedding ready at home. Remember that this is the first day in your puppy's life that he will be without his littermates, and it may be his first day without his mom. It is a *big* day.

Crate Training

You will need a crate for your new arrival. I usually start with a small crate and move up to a bigger one. If your breeder does not loan you a "baby" crate, a crate can be inexpensively purchased at a discount store. I use plastic airline crates in winter and wire crates in summer. A plastic crate is easier to clean (especially if the

pup makes a mistake). A small crate is cozy for the new arrival, and encourages faster housetraining, as the crate is not big enough to encourage the puppy to go off in a corner to relieve himself. Several nylon fleece pads will also be needed. They wash and dry in a flash. Puppies make mistakes, but all dogs naturally want a clean environment. Keeping his crate clean will encourage your pup to wait to go outside to do his business.

Teach your puppy to sleep in a crate and to go there when asked. You will need "time out" as you raise a Shorthair. A crate is a way to keep your mental

A crate offers a puppy a cozy place that is his alone.

health, household order and your puppy safe when not under strict observation. The crate should be a safe place for the puppy to go. Many breeders introduce several crates to the puppy play area before the pups are ready to leave for new homes, so that they are used to going into them in the play yard when they are tired.

Put the crate next to your bed for the first several nights until the pup is over any anxiety of leaving the litter. If he awakens during the night, you can hear him and take him out for a bathroom break. Few puppies can make it the whole night through at first. When he returns to his crate, a calming voice and a hand on the top of the crate can comfort him. It is best to limit water intake after six at night until the puppy gets through the night and seems to be waiting to go outside until morning.

Housetraining

Housetrain by whisking the pup outdoors immediately when he comes out of the crate or looks like he is sniffing around urgently. When he goes outside where you want him to go, praise him. If he makes a mistake, say nothing. Do not scold, shriek or be urgent. Simply pick up the pup and place him out of doors. When he does what you want, be jolly about it. Teach all things with positive enforcement. Ignore unwanted behavior or interrupt it, replace it with wanted behavior, then enforce it. Stay happy and upbeat if you want a well-adjusted Shorthair. They are more sensitive than you might think.

The best way to enjoy your Shorthair puppy during housetraining is to be sure he has a fenced yard that is readily accessible by a convenient house door. Shorthairs get busy and, like active children, suddenly "discover" they need to go out to relieve themselves. Your new dog will run to the door and fling his puppy self against it. If you have not prepared a fenced enclosure and have to pick up the pup to take him out or go find a leash, you may be too late. Housetraining will take longer if you have not prepared an enclosure. Remember that this enclosure is only to keep your Shorthair from running off faster than you can catch him. Do not leave him out unobserved or alone. Shorthairs are happy diggers, and they climb, so be observant.

Puppy-Proofing

Before you bring your puppy home, look around for the items you cherish that might entice the puppy. Put them away. Leather-bound books, magazines, your shoes, the laundry, objects on coffee tables, baskets. Now you are getting the idea. Check your houseplants, and put them up high. Some houseplants, including English ivy, philodendron and many ferns and Poinsettia, are toxic to dogs. Outdoor plants that are listed as toxic include rhododendrons, but get a list for your area from the state agricultural department. Shorthairs are resistant to many toxic plants, so they may show no sign of harm unless they ingest a large quantity of the plant. It is still better to know which ones to look out for.

Toxic chemicals are also a problem in the household. Secure items like soap, medications and cleaning agents out of harm's way. In the garage, make sure that all poisons, gardening fertilizers and chemicals are locked away.

Keep a young dog confined in a safe room—washable floors are strongly advised!

Antifreeze tastes good to a dog, but it is highly toxic and will kill your pet, so be sure that he cannot get near it.

Start the puppy in a single room of the house. The kitchen is good for easy cleanup. If you need to use baby gates to fence off the room, get them ahead of time. We built accordion-folding Dutch doors between our kitchen and living room. They open and fold neatly into the wall when not in use, and make a Shorthair proof barrier when wet paws are unwanted on the oriental carpets. The open upper Dutch section allows us to see what puppy is doing, but you can close it to offer yourself or the pup quiet time.

You will also want to secure all electrical appliances, especially heaters and cords, and be sure a fireplace or wood stove will not harm the puppy. Attractive screens are available to keep children safe from these hazards, and they are equally useful for your Shorthair baby.

Toys

Shorthairs love toys. A soft-mouthed retriever by nature, a Shorthair will spend much of the day carrying something in his mouth, usually something soft.

Give your Shorthair his own soft toys. Stuffed animals work, but your pup does not recognize his stuffed animals as cute, so you can make inexpensive nylon fleece toys yourself in pillow and ball shapes. They work just as well, and they have no hard button eyes or noses to tear out and swallow or leave around the room. Toys will last longer if they do not have eyes to pull out and start the endless removal of stuffing. Many days I have come into a living room where the carpet and chairs looked snow-covered from toy stuffing. Teach your pup to retrieve toys. It is another form of mastery and bonding, and Shorthairs are natural, happy retrievers.

POOR TOY CHOICES

Do not make the mistake of giving your puppy or adoptive dog your old socks or old tennis shoes. Shorthairs love the personal objects of their owners because they smell like you, and they must learn quickly that all personal items of owners are off-limits. If you let them have one thing that smells like you, they will collect dozens of others—your eyeglasses, credit cards, wallet, costly handbag, shoes, underwear and nylon panty hose. They may even carry some of the more embarrassing items on this list out in front of houseguests. Worse yet, nylon hose are easily swallowed and do not move through the digestive tract without doing damage. Many a costly emergency surgery has exposed ingested undergarments, a few household sponges, some steel wool, a rubber sink stopper and a set of rubber gloves. You will want to prevent this tendency to take your things by giving your Shorthair many of his own. It will be worth it in the long run.

CHEW TOYS

There is some controversy over whether or not to allow Shorthairs rawhide bones and sticks to chew. We have never had a problem with either, and would have a very hard time stopping our Shorthairs from gathering, fetching and chewing sticks, as they have a woodlot as part of their yard. I buy good quality rawhide to prevent potential danger of chemicals used in processing that might hurt the dogs, and these do keep them busy on rainy days. Other choices professionals recommend are nylon bones that slough off tiny particles of nylon as the dogs chew, and these pass easily through the digestive tract. There are now natural cornstarch bones for sale in pet supply stores, and rubber Kong toys with a little cheese or peanut butter applied to the inside can keep a puppy busy for some time.

The value of a good chew toy should not be underestimated.

Treats

We occasionally give pups hard puppy biscuits made of natural ingredients for training and tooth cleaning. Make the puppy learn something to get a treat every time, and remember to limit treats to avoid a plump Shorthair in adulthood. Some people also give occasional raw knuckle bones to their dogs, and we have done so also. As our dogs live in the house with us, however, this is a bit messy for the living room. They also get buried in some curious places in our yard. For our older dogs and those with a tendency to gain weight, we feed raw baby carrots as training treats.

"Treats" to avoid at all costs are chocolate and cooked bones. Chocolate is toxic to dogs. Cooked bones can splinter in your dog's mouth and can be very dangerous to your Shorthair's health. Keep the Halloween candy and the bones away from your dog.

Shorthair Supplies

COLLARS AND LEASHES

A simple, adjustable, flat nylon collar with a flat brass plate with your phone number on it will do. Because you will not want to traumatize your puppy, you will want to teach him to follow you without a leash in a safe place before you ever use a leash as a lead. Once the puppy is leash comfortable, I use retractable leashes to give exercise outside of the fenced area or when traveling, and a 6-foot leather obedience lead for short recalls, leash walking and moderate obedience training.

We do not use chain choke collars, but if your obedience instructor elects to use them, be sure that the puppy is never on a choke collar of any kind when you are not on the other end of the leash. These collars can catch on branches or protruding objects, and the puppy can hang himself.

DOGGY DISHES

I recommend stainless steel food bowls for Shorthairs. Stainless steel is easy to clean (can be popped in the dishwasher) and is quite sanitary. I use the 3-quart size. I use a pottery water bowl, as it is heavy enough to be stable when the dogs drink from it. You can get both in most dog catalogs, pet shops or farm stores. I do not use plastic bowls, as the chemicals in the plastic tend to turn the pup's nose leather a lighter color.

Home Alone

Before leaving puppies or adult dogs for any period of time, I generally try to tire them out. Then I offer them a frustrating chew toy, such as a commercially prepared marrowbone from the dog store stuffed down in the middle with hard cheddar cheese. I crate the pup, and give him the marrowbone. This toy is only given when I am going out and the pup needs

> **APPROPRIATE EXERCISE**
>
> If you want to jog with your Shorthair, wait until the puppy is 1 year old and his bones are fully formed. Pounding on his joints when they are just forming is not good for them. Frisbee, ball fetch and hide and seek may have to do until he gets older.

something to occupy him until he tires of the task and falls off to sleep. When marrowbone is not in use, we refrigerate it.

WORKING NINE-TO-FIVE

If you work outside of the home, I recommend a mid-day visit from a dog care provider, a drop off at a dog day care center, a safe, warm kennel with a fellow dog or a secure outdoor yard with lots of things to do and where barking is not an issue with neighbors.

I often leave on a television or radio for my Shorthairs when I am out, especially when I have puppies in the house. A fellow breeder in Washington State leaves cartoons on when she is away from her pups working during the day, as it gets her puppies used to the voices of little children. If you have no small children, but want to be sure your puppy grows up unafraid of them, why not try cartoons?

KEEP YOUR ARRIVALS MELLOW

If you can distract your puppy from thinking about your departure or your return, he will experience less anxiety, and be better adjusted. Try not to make much out of leaving or coming home. Do a few obedience commands before crating or when coming back home before any effusive greeting or enthusiastic play.

A COMPANION DOG?

If the Shorthair is eventually to be alone a lot, some people have been tempted to get two at once. Do not do this. If you do, it is likely that the puppies will bond with one another and become less bonded and less attentive to their human family.

GOOD FENCING IS A MUST

If you are committing to a Shorthair, commit to fencing. You will be happier, and the dog healthier, in the long run.

If you are planning on electronic fencing (suitable for dogs 5 months and older) you will benefit from putting up temporary garden fencing you can get at a farm or hardware store until the pup is ready for the electronic fence. This also gives children and adults an outdoor space where they can play safely with the puppy. Chaining or using cable ties with trolleys are not suitable for Shorthairs. This is an energetic sporting dog that does a lot of jumping in play and that can be seriously injured on a tie out.

Some people have found success in getting a second dog once the pup has bonded to the family and learned some rules. The ideal solution is to get an older dog that is used to other dogs. Also make sure that the adoptive dog has had experience living with the other inhabitants of your home, be they children, cats or birds. To locate an older dog, try contacting German Shorthaired Pointer Rescue. As an alternative, a breeder might have a returned dog, a show or field prospect that is ready to retire or a dog that did not compete well. If he keeps his dogs in the household and not in kennels, he may be a good source for a second dog.

Puppy Training

When you get your puppy, you will need to set aside a time twice or three times a day for what I like to call formal training. At first, this will be training to follow, hide and seek, hide and find the object and bring-it-to-me games. Actually, you are teaching mastery, come when called, basic hunting skills and retrieving, but it is all lots of fun and puppyhood should be just that. For more on training basics, see chapter 8. In the case of a hunting dog, however, and particularly in the case of the Shorthair, which is an intense hunting dog, some extra tips may be valuable.

The hard part is teaching your puppy not to pick something up.

First, teaching your dog to come when called must be started early, and it must not be negotiable. Second, a Shorthair must learn to leave a thing alone when you do not want him to mouth it, pick it up, chase it or show interest in it. This may sound easy, but a dog with an intense prey drive by nature will not willingly relinquish the object of his interest. Begin training when the dog is young, by placing enticing things in his way and teaching him to leave them alone or to wait for them.

EARLY HUNTING PREPARATION

If you plan to hunt with your Shorthair, start to prepare him when he is a puppy. Be sure that a lot of commotion accompanies feeding time, then he learns not to be fearful of loud noises, lots of people, new situations and surprises. Take him out and socialize him as much as possible.

A puppy should only be fired over after he has been exposed to large numbers of birds and is too excited about them to care about the sound of a gun. Some people choose to accustom their dogs to gunshots by using a starter pistol when the pups are eating, when some wonderful play situation has developed or when the pup gets excited around the bird pen at the hunting preserve or training center. There are many good books and tapes on gun dog training available from the American Kennel Club. It is best to refer to published advice and tapes when you are starting out. Well-meaning friends and acquaintances may not have the skill and knowledge that you need.

Most importantly, *do not* presume you can take a Shorthair out the first season and shoot over him with no prior bird experience or training. That is a sure path to creating a sound-shy and gun-shy dog. Gun-shy dogs are created, not born. Part of your preparation in having a happy and successful relationship with a Shorthair is knowing what not to do until the puppy is ready, and until you are knowledgeable enough to train your dog effectively.

chapter 5

Feeding

Your German

Shorthaired Pointer

"Ever consider what they must think of us? I mean here we come back from a grocery store with the most amazing haul—chicken, pork, half a cow. They must think we are the greatest hunters on earth!"

—Ann Tyler

The most important advice I can give is that you must pay attention to the dog's health, energy level, coat and skin condition, breath and tooth tartar to give you signals about whether you are feeding "the right stuff." What is right for one German Shorthaired Pointer may not be quite right for another. Find a veterinarian with whom you feel trust and comfort, and who understands the pros and cons of all of these positions on dog food and can talk with you about them intelligently. That way the decision is a learning process, and you will think it through yourself with an eye on the health and condition of your dog.

This is a muscular, athletic, high-energy breed that tends to burn a lot of calories, and canines have a much shorter, "hotter" digestive tract than humans do.

The canine digestive tract is designed for what dogs would find to eat if they were still running in wild packs—that is, meat, raw meat. It is my opinion that a dog should eat as naturally as possible, bearing in mind the owner's ability to make that food. If we watch wild canids, we will see that they hunt prey, do a little foraging and are not too fussy about whether dinner is fresh. If you choose to prepare fresh food for your dogs, there are many good books that can provide you with some handy recipes.

Commercial Dry Foods

If you choose, as do most people, to use a commercial dry dog food, learning to read the label and learning to read your Shorthair for signs of good health are equally important. You should take some confidence, however, in the fact that most of the major dog food companies spend fathoms of money and research time formulating and testing dog foods to satisfy dogs and their owners. Whatever your prejudices about ingredients, you should be able to find a suitable commercial food.

Understanding Labels

Reading the dog food bag is the first step in your education. The section labeled "Ingredients" is where you start. All you really need to know is that the first ingredient listed is the largest single ingredient in the bag by weight. If that is wheat or corn or beet pulp, then meat is not the primary ingredient in the dog food. If the first ingredient says some form of meat, followed by the word "meal," then the meat component is not all muscle meat. The Shorthair is a dog that uses high-quality protein efficiently. Foods that contain muscle meat as a first ingredient are good choices for this breed.

There is a lot of controversy about several dog food issues: fat preservatives, protein level and flavor enhancers. Many people avoid such fat preservatives in their Shorthair's food such as BHT, BHA and Ethoxyquin. These chemicals have been used for many decades as fat preservatives, and have only recently come under scrutiny. People who do not wish to feed products with artificial fat preservatives in them choose foods preserved with vitamin C and E as fat preservatives. Be aware that fat preservatives extend the shelf life of your dog food, so look for the food expiration date regardless of what you choose.

The active Shorthair will benefit from a food containing high-quality protein.

Protein

In the case of high performance foods for dogs hard at work most of the time or field trialing, protein level ranges from percentages in the high teens to above thirty. There are many differing opinions regarding the best level of protein for active sporting dogs. I use food with a protein level of 24 percent for my young and active dogs, and a senior food of the same brand with a protein level of 18 percent for my old and less active Shorthairs who also tend to put on weight too easily. I supplement for dogs needing more protein with raw meat and flaxseed or flaxseed oil, garlic, kelp and sometimes a commercial supplement. I keep a close eye on my dogs and shift food and supplements if I see changes that warrant a dietary change.

Taste Enhancers

The most common taste enhancer is on the label as "poultry digest." This is what is left over from the poultry that is not considered suited for human consumption. It is sprayed on the food to make it tasty. Dogs consider it to be so, as dogs have very little "taste" according to human thinking. Still, it seems to work for most dogs. If you are sensitive to what your dog eats, look for products with garlic and other seemingly more palatable additions in them. Garlic is not only tasty, but many contemporary canine nutritionists think it is health enhancing.

A lustrous coat and healthy skin are signs that you are feeding your dog right.

HEALTHFUL ADDITIONS TO A COMMERCIAL FOOD

Just because you have chosen a dry dog food, it does not mean you cannot add other foods to enhance health and well-being. A chunk of raw meat every few days keeps a Shorthair's natural enzymes working, and is an easy natural supplement to the diet. I ask my hunter friends to supply me with surplus game, freeze it for three to six months to ensure parasites are not a threat and supplement with it. Game has less chance of pesticide, antibiotic and hormone levels that might impact my Shorthair's health profile.

DRY FOOD FADS

While there has been a trend toward lamb and rice foods in the '90s, there is no reason that lamb or rice is a superior combination to any other protein carbohydrate mix. When some dogs developed food allergies in the past, veterinarians would move them from beef, chicken or some other meat to lamb, and from corn, wheat or soy to rice. Changing the food for a time would remove the allergen, and thus the skin condition caused by it. It is just as likely if the dog involved started out on lamb and rice food, that she would have developed an allergy to that and have to be moved to another, more traditional food. Do not be inclined to switch from one fad food to another. Find a regimen that suits your dog and you and stick to it. The skin is the window to the Shorthair's well-being. Health shows on the surface, and good food is one key to good health.

Feeding Frequency

If, for example, their main staple is field mice, dogs in the wild will tend to eat frequently, but they will eat less often if they have taken larger game. The household companion Shorthair should eat three meals a day until 6 months of age to aid development, weight support and digestion. If you get a puppy, you should feed her the same food that she was fed by the breeder. For that first several months she should eat all she wants as long as she does not get fat. She is in the throes of growing constantly, and will look thin one moment and round the next. At 6 months of age, start feeding two meals a

Until she reaches 6 months of age, a puppy should be given three meals a day.

day for the rest of the dog's life. The commercial dog food instructions on amounts of food to feed are only averages, and they are not breed specific. A Shorthair is an energetic athlete and as a rule, she will require more food than a breed that is inactive.

Timing Meals

It is better to roust the dog, let her go outside for a bit, return to the house and settle a little before feeding. Shorthairs that are fed immediately on getting up or when you arrive home in the evening, for example, get too pushy about food. Once you have fed, allow the dog to settle again for a time before heavy exercise. Feeding a full meal

just before exercise can bring on a bloating condition in long-bodied, deep-chested dogs. The Shorthair can be both, and bloat and a torsion, or twisted stomach, can be fatal.

Treats

I do not believe an owner should feed table scraps or indiscriminate treats or junk food to Shorthairs. By doing so, you encourage your Shorthair to become a beggar, and she will not leave you alone if you are eating. While this may be acceptable for people living alone, guests may not look on it so favorably. In addition, two measured meals a day keep you in control of your Shorthair's nutrition. You can add or subtract the amount you are feeding easily, and if you think the dog is experiencing a food allergy, identifying the potential causes is simpler. The most important reasons to avoid giving your dog table scraps, however, are that she may either get fat or she may become a picky eater with daily changes in what is added to her food.

Some people feed commercial dog treats that they buy in the market, and if you limit those treats to training devices, I see nothing wrong with it. I would recommend, however, that you look carefully at the ingredients on the package and be sure that what you are giving your dog is what you would want her to eat. It is far better to throw some meat in the microwave oven or give your dog baby carrots and beans as training treats than use something with ingredients that leave you wondering. There is no reason to sabotage the dog's proper daily ration by filling her up with chemicals with unpronounceable names between meals.

Some people start their puppies with a limited time in which to eat. This is the right approach for adult dogs.

Picky Pointers

Although I have been breeding purebred dogs since the age of 10, my first home-bred German Shorthaired Pointer show puppy blessed my life only a dozen years ago. I was like every other proud, indulgent, hovering show puppy owner. I spoiled her. When I wanted her to gain weight for the show ring, I would feed her any-thing experienced show handlers advised. We fed mac-aroni and cheese, roasted chicken, steak with the fat left on. If you can imagine it, we probably tried it.

If you have a Shorthair who gets fussy about food for whatever reason, stop encouraging this behavior. Take a bowl of dry dog food (it is best to leave it dry so it won't spoil), and take the dog to the kennel or other confined space. Put the dog in the kennel, make sure she has lots of water and put down her dish. Leave the dish there for ten or twenty minutes of time where she is not easily distracted. If she does not eat, pick up the food. The next meal, do the same thing with the same food. I guarantee, within two or three days she will start eating normally again. Don't start spoiling her again if you can help it, but if you do, return to this regimen.

By feeding mea-sured, regular meals, you retain control over your dog's diet.

Some people call this the "windows" or limited time ap-proach to feeding, and start even puppies off this way. I believe that your dog's health, training, bonding—and whatever you ask your Shorthair to do—will be more successful if you feed for a limited amount of time and pick up the food. I do not recommend leaving the bowl down all day for self-feeding. Doing so can create picky, inefficient eaters or fat Shorthairs, and a sport-ing dog should be fit—not fat.

Weight Watching

Fat is a problem with many companion Shorthairs if they are neutered, have limited running time, as they age, if they are injured or if owners replace the time they should be spending with their active sporting dog with food. I call this "guilt feeding." Once the Shorthair is fat, there are a number of ways to bring her back to a normal weight.

EXERCISE

If you have a fat dog, exercise is the best first step. Slowly build up the cardiovascular workout in a really obese and aged dog. We are looking for increased health here, not a coronary.

A dog at the correct weight will be lean and hard-muscled.

BREAK OUT THE VEGGIES

Make sure lots of water is available at all times, and break out the vegetables. The length and heat of the digestive tract in a dog makes fully digesting raw vegetative material inefficient. Most will pass through the animal without giving much value—and very few calories.

Use carrots and green beans ground in a food processor and blend with a very small portion of senior dog food. Feed baby carrots whenever you need to give a treat.

Supplement with a general-purpose doggy vitamin and a half-teaspoon of flaxseed oil daily to make skin and coat glow.

IS YOUR SHORTHAIR STOCKY?

The Shorthair should look like a hard-muscled, athletic hunting dog. With the dog standing, you should be able to discern two or three of the rear or floating ribs on a mature Shorthair. The backbone and hipbones should not be prominent, but a sure sign of a Shorthair too fat is an indentation, or "dimple" just in front of the tail origin. If your Shorthair has such a dimple at any age, take some weight off of her.

> **TO SUPPLEMENT OR NOT TO SUPPLEMENT?**
>
> If you're feeding your dog a diet that's correct for her developmental stage and she's alert, healthy-looking and neither over- nor underweight, you don't need to add supplements. These include table scraps as well as vitamins and minerals. In fact, a growing puppy is in danger of developing muscu-loskeletal disorders by oversupple-mentation. If you have any concerns about the nutritional quality of the food you're feeding, discuss them with your veterinarian.

How to Know that You're Feeding Right

As you decide how to feed your Shorthair, remember that weight, coat condition, energy level, attitude and enthusiasm are the best signs that you are doing the right thing. Bad breath, excess stool volume, weight loss, dull coat and eyes and sudden lethargy may indicate onslaught of illness, but they may also indicate that you need to look at your feeding and nutritional practices and make a change. Remember to change one thing at a time until you see that bloom of good health and high energy return to your Shorthair.

chapter 6

Grooming
Your German Shorthaired
Pointer

"I wonder if other dogs think poodles are members of a weird religious cult."
—Rita Rudner

One of the reasons you probably considered getting a Shorthair is because the breed is often thought of as a "dust and run" dog. This is basically true. The most frequent questions I get about the breed, however, are "Do they shed?" and "Will they cause allergic reactions in people allergic to dogs?" The answer to both of these questions is "yes."

Shedding

Shorthairs shed just as much as other dogs shed, and do it more profusely in the spring and fall of the year, if you live in a four-season climate. They do, however, seem to shed less than other dogs because their hair is often shorter than half an inch. Regular bathing and grooming can make this shedding seem even more insignificant.

Allergies

Most allergic reactions to pets are not to their hair at all, but to the sloughing of the skin, or dander. Because Shorthairs have little coat, the dander can be bathed or groomed away easily, and people with minor allergies to dogs may find a Shorthair tolerable. People with more severe allergies will not.

Make the bath a pleasant experience—take your dog inside and use warm water in the tub.

Bathing

Bathing is simple. I do not recommend using a garden hose and cold water, unless you want Stu the Shorthair to fear the hose and being bathed. Take him inside, to the tub, and have your towels and shampoo ready. Make sure the water is tepid and that you have a hose with a shower attachment for wetting and rinsing. Gradually wet the dog, turn off the water and work in the shampoo. Your breeder, veterinarian or local pet supply store can recommend a good quality pet shampoo.

I bathe my Shorthairs more often than many people do, I am sure. I show them, and the dogs being actively campaigned get bathed once a week before going to shows. This would indicate that bathing does not hurt their coats or skin, but I supplement with flax-seed oil to be sure the coat and skin have sufficient oil.

To minimize shedding and obtain a coat that looks and feels great, bathe your dog in the hottest water that he will tolerate. Bathe as frequently as possible so long that the coat and skin are not harmed. During the summer months, my dogs swim in my pool at will, so I use minimum pool chemicals and do not bathe my Shorthairs as regularly in summer.

A Shorthair's coat should, if you remember the breed standard, be harsh to the touch, so I do not use conditioners, but if the dog is not hunted, softening the coat with a conditioner will not harm anything. Be sure you examine every area of the dog with the shampoo massaging during the bath. Not only is this important bonding time, it is also a good time to examine your dog for an injury. (You will also want to look for ticks and signs of flea infestation, discussed more thoroughly in chapter 7.)

Should you find a minor cut or scrape, apply an antiseptic to the area. Shorthairs may be more prone to minor skin injury than heavier coated dogs, but they are surely more prone to injury because they are a bit reckless when they run through yards, woods and fields. They are not very pain sensitive when they play, so they may not look at you soulfully and hold up a leg for your inspection until a long time after the injury has occurred. Be sure to check the pads of the feet when you bathe as well. It is not unusual for them to be injured on sharp rocks, broken glass, thorns or metal when Shorthairs run full out.

DRYING

Drying time can be one of the most enjoyable times you have with your Shorthair. They love being toweled and will often play with the towel while you are rubbing their coat dry. I take the back of a common comb and run it in the direction the hair grows to strip out excess water before towel drying. Some of my dogs enjoy the hair dryer, and it cuts drying time in half. In the summer, wet dogs can just go outside to finish drying, but in the winter, keep them in until they are no longer damp.

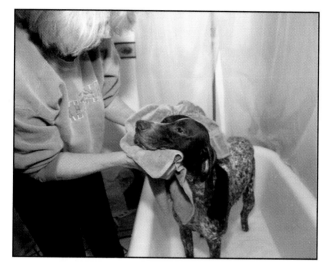

Shorthairs enjoy being toweled dry. A post-bath rub down is a nice way to bond with your dog.

Brushing

A good Shorthair coat is so tight that common dog brushes will not be of much value. For brushing Shorthairs, I recommend a rubber glove with tiny rubber teeth on it, (usually used to groom a horse). These gloves can be inexpensively purchased at any feed or tack store. There are a number of other rubber brushes that work well; again, most are designed for use on horses. Rubber grabs the short, close coat and pulls the loose hair away from the growing hair better than a conventional brush. I brush once every day or two during heavy shedding periods, and I do it outdoors. There is no reason to clip a Shorthair.

At other times of the year, I may only occasionally rub down the dog with a towel. In winter, particularly when preparing for holiday visitors or houseguests, I put the upholstery nozzle on the vacuum and

*A rubber glove
with tiny teeth is
a great tool for
brushing the
Shorthair's dense
coat.*

vacuum the dogs. Some dogs will be sensitive to the vacuum, so start getting them used to playing with the nozzle in the presence of the sound when they are quite young.

Eye and Ear Care

The coat is not the only part of a dog that needs grooming. Wipe any weeping or discharge away from the eyes regularly with a soft cloth or tissue. Any floppy-eared dog requires regular ear cleaning. A foul odor from the ear(s) indicates an ear infection, and if you detect an unpleasant odor, see your veterinarian. Wipe out the ears with a soft cloth, tissue or a perfume-free baby wipe. If your Shorthair swims or retrieves out of water, remember to dry inside his ears after he swims. For the novice, I do not recommend using cotton swabs for ear cleaning. There is too much danger of ear injury by cleaning too deeply or roughly.

Nail Care

Grooming your pup's nails should have already begun before you brought him home. Your breeder should have cut the pup's nails several times while he was still nursing to prevent those tiny sharp nails from making the mother sore as the pups push on her to stimulate milk production. I recommend weekly nail care from birth through life.

Few Shorthairs do the work they were bred for. If they do not hunt or run on fairly hard ground regularly, they will need their nails groomed. The hard footpads accompanied by thick, tough nails make running all day over rough terrain possible. Without this use, nails can grow too long and spread a dog's toes, making the feet unsound. If you can hear your Shorthair's nails click on a hard floor surface, they need grooming.

You may use a nail clipper, a motorized grinder or a heavy file. I usually cut nails with a nail clipper if they have gotten longer than usual, and then smooth them off with a file or grinder. Once they are at correct length, using a grinder once a week will keep Shorthair nails in check.

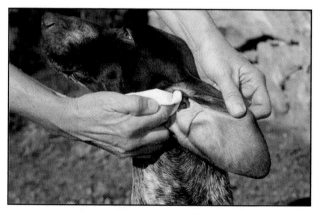

Wipe out ears with a soft cloth.

Get Your Dog Accustomed to Clipping

Sit on a comfortable cushion on the floor, and put the dog or pup on his back, head toward you, with his feet in the air. When you first do this, you will have to make the dog comfortable in this position. The first clipping should be very minor, being sure not to cut the quick of the nail. Normally, you can see a slight indentation on the underside of the nail where the sharp part of the nail to be removed meets the heavier body of the nail. Stop trimming before you reach the body of the nail.

Ask your breeder, a groomer or a friend who has done this before to demonstrate for you before your first try at trimming. If you begin by using a grinder, and you do so regularly, you will not have to worry about injury, as the heat of the grinding tool causes the quick to recede somewhat each time it is used.

Tooth Care

Some people feed their dogs hard-baked dog biscuits every so often to remove plaque from teeth. If you are going to do this, do be sure the ingredients are healthy, nutritious and chemical free. Others use hard nylon chew toys or softer gum toys with protrusions to clean the teeth while the dog chews. Some rope bone toys are made of nylon floss, and are advertised for tooth cleaning. Chewing hard surfaces does help keep teeth healthy.

It's easy to clean your Shorthair's teeth with a rubber fingertip brush.

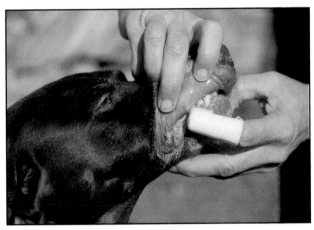

If plaque and tartar still build up, you may need to use a rubber fingertip brush or occasionally scrape the teeth with a metal tooth scraper. Most people have this done on veterinary visits, if it is needed, or they have a thorough hydrosonic cleaning done at any time the dog needs to be under anesthesia.

As any healthy Shorthair may only be under anesthesia once in his life for neuter surgery, sustaining healthy teeth is a matter of seeing that your Shorthair has some healthy chewing to do, and gets an occasional manual cleaning and inspection from you or your veterinarian.

Keeping Your
German
Shorthaired Pointer
Healthy

"A dog is the only thing on this earth that loves you more than he loves himself." —Josh Billings (Henry Wheeler Shaw) 1818–1885

Start with a Healthy Dog

The best advice I can give on keeping your Shorthair healthy is to encourage you to know enough to select a healthy one in the first place. Intelligent ownership is the best advantage a Shorthair can have.

The advice I have already offered to you on choosing a breeder and being sure heritable health checks have been given to both sire and dam of the litter you have selected will give you a good start in keeping your Shorthair healthy throughout life.

73

Don't Worry, Be Happy

The primary underlying cause for illness in dogs—from skin conditions to cancer—is a compromised immune system. Although there are some Shorthairs that have less hardy immune systems than others, you, the owner, can do a very great deal to support and build the immune system. The most important health care you can provide is preventative health care. This starts with the right diet, exercise, positive, stress-free training, a protected temperate place to sleep and be safe and an intelligent, dedicated and loving family. The dog's mental health and sense of well-being will impact her health.

Plenty of love, fresh air, exercise and the out-of-doors bolsters a Shorthair's well-being. Perhaps one of the best things you can do to keep your Shorthair healthy is, simply enough, to keep her happy. It may seem odd to say that happiness is health care, and may help prevent an early death from a disease like cancer, but many health professionals, including veterinarians, are beginning to see some logic in

Get your Short-hair outside and spend time with your dog. A happy dog is a healthy dog!

this. A perpetually lonely Shorthair is not happy, nor is one who is frustrated by lack of exercise or interest, nor one that is shut away from the world most of the time. The best preventative medicine you can give your Shorthair just may be joy. It can't hurt.

When Your Dog Is Ailing

You will be able to tell if your Shorthair is developing a health problem when you see a significant change in the bouncy, glowing, energetic, food-motivated Shorthair you started with. A listless Shorthair is unnatural.

A Shorthair that will not eat may not be telling you she has already eaten. If her eyes suddenly seem dull, or if her coat dulls and you see flaking skin in the coat, something is going wrong. Of course, diarrhea and/or vomiting indicate that you need to watch the dog carefully, try to figure out what she has recently eaten, or if she has a virus causing this behavior.

EXAMINE YOUR DOG

Examine your dog for wounds or pests whenever you groom her. If you detect a growth, and you know it is not merely a wart in an aging Shorthair, it is best to check with your veterinarian. If a lump grows quickly, it may be malignant. There are growths we call "fatty tumors" which, however unsightly they may become, are not health risks. Some people prefer to leave them

Run your hands regularly over your dog to feel for any injuries.

alone rather than risk general anesthesia—itself a health risk— to remove the benign tumor. Ask your veterinarian about local anesthesia for minor lumps and bumps.

As you clip or grind nails every week or two, be sure to look for infection, irritation or injury around the base of the nails. If you find something minor, a topical antibiotic will probably clear it up. If it looks more serious, see your veterinarian.

If your Shorthair is scratching or pawing at eyes or ears, or if there is excessive discharge from eyes or ears or foul-smelling ears, a more serious problem is on the horizon. Deal with it promptly.

The basic philosophy I hold is that the eyes, ears and skin and behavior of the dog are health barometers. The most important thing you can do as an owner is pay attention, and act on what you see right away without being an alarmist.

Weight Watching

There are some basics for all dogs that also apply to the Shorthair. Proper feeding has already discussed in chapter 5, but I would emphasize here that an obese Shorthair, or an emaciated one, is vulnerable when other diseases assault her. Both extremes can also indicate an underlying problem that is more serious than mere over- or underfeeding. If your Shorthair does not gain weight no matter how much you feed her, and no matter how many times you try a new ration, you should see your veterinarian. Some illnesses prevent weight gain. This is also true with obesity in a young dog. All dogs have somewhat different metabolisms, just like people, but a very obese young dog may be at the outset of a serious illness.

Health Profile of the Breed

Bright, clear eyes are a sign of good health.

In all, the German Shorthaired Pointer is considered a healthy dog with long life expectancy. Unfortunately, there are some maladies that are passed on genetically, and you should have an awareness of them.

HIP DYSPLASIA

Even with all the best precautions, there are occasional cases of hip dysplasia in Shorthairs. But note that the fitness, athleticism and muscular strength of a Shorthair will often mask even this disorder until extreme old age.

VON WILLEBRAND'S DISEASE

Von Willebrand's Disease is a bleeding disorder inherited in German Shorthaired Pointers, but in my quarter century living with this breed, I have yet to see a single case. One can screen for this disease, and if you decide to do so, be sure to have the blood tested by the most sophisticated means available in order to ensure that you receive an accurate reading. Consult with your veterinarian about testing for this disorder.

EYE DISORDERS

Juvenile cataracts have been found in Shorthairs, but they seldom result in blindness. There is a rare, heritable day blindness, but I have only heard of three cases, and these were all in the same family of dogs. Other eye disorders are minor and do not seem to impair the dog's function as a companion. Nonetheless, eye certification should be a requirement for breeding.

Minor heart murmurs are not uncommon in Shorthair pups, but most puppies outgrow this condition.

HEART DISEASE

There are several major heart ailments seen in the breed, among them subaortic stenosis (SAS) and mitral valve disease. Both are heritable, which is one reason for heart certification. Many young pups will exhibit a minor grade one or two heart murmur, but most puppies outgrow these early life minor murmurs. Even if they do not, murmurs not associated with SAS or mitral valve are seldom a serious inconvenience, even in a dog that occasionally hunts. A more prominent murmur, above grade two, should be taken more seriously.

OTHER BREED MALADIES

Occasional cases of Addison's disease and Cushing's disease (both an abnormal production of adrenal hormones) are found in Shorthairs. Shorthairs may also

77

*As is evident,
you will need a
tall fence to prop-
erly confine your
Shorthair.*

suffer from demodectic mange, which may indicate a downturn in the immune system, skin irritations and allergies. It is, overall, however, a healthy breed.

Good Fences Make Good Health

If you have selected a healthy offspring from a healthy family of dogs, you are now responsible for keeping the dog healthy for the rest of her life. The most common cause of death among German Shorthaired Pointers is being hit by cars. This is not a disease, of course, but it is often terminal and can be prevented by proper

containment and proper training in addition to owner vigilance. It is silly to say that you cannot afford proper fencing for your Shorthair when the lack of it will cost you your dog, or an even larger amount of money for a veterinary repair of injury and broken limbs. If you commit to the breed, commit to its proper containment, training and care.

CONVENTIONAL FENCING

Conventional fencing is appropriate for a Shorthair, but only if it is secured underground at the base to prevent digging out, if the containment material will withstand a Shorthair's will to escape, and if it is tall enough to prevent jumping over. Shorthairs are not eager to be left alone, and will try to get to where there is company, another dog or a bird of any kind. They are very determined once they have started a project.

ELECTRONIC FENCING

Some Shorthairs that could not be contained in conventional fencing have succeeded on electronic or "invisible fencing." Electronic fencing will work if the training process is correct and thorough. Make sure that the dog is tested with "proofs" or tantalizing lures across the fence just to be sure the training is really complete. This is not something to rush.

Some people think that electronic fencing is cruel because it shocks the dog. In truth, if the dog is trained properly, she receives several mild shocks during the training process as enforcers. These are harmless, but convincing. The rest of her life, if the owner remembers to change the collar battery, she will only be reminded that she is too near the fence by an audible electronic signal. Imagine how much more cruel it is to allow your sporting dog to run free and be hit by a vehicle.

I have had five or six Shorthairs, both male and female, some neutered, some not, on my electronic fence system for more than a dozen years. Not once have we had any of our dogs roam away. Proper training is key to the success of electronic fencing. Do your homework, and be sure the training is done right. You will save your dog's life.

Be aware that electronic fencing is not designed to contain your dog when you are away from home and she is outside alone, nor does it inhibit other dogs from coming on your property.

Health and Veterinarians

A person who breeds, engages in any sort of performance or competition and does rescue with Shorthairs is likely to practice some minor medical care. I keep a powdered anesthetic/antibiotic on hand for minor cuts, worm my dogs myself, treat minor diarrhea and simple upset stomach. I have even been known to take a stitch or two when far away from help. The pet Shorthair owner will not be likely to need the veterinarian much, but when you do, having chosen the right one will put you at ease.

CHOOSING A VET

First, be sure you know and respect your veterinarian's credentials. You must trust the veterinarian, and it would be a fine thing if your Shorthair did, too. Wrestling with a 70-pound Shorthair who does not want a stranger to "look at" her can be tense. It is nice to like your veterinarian, but trust and respect are more important to your dog's health. What is also important is that the veterinarian likes the breed. If the veterinarian makes jokes or disparaging remarks about the breed in general, or if he is ill at ease with your dog, it is best for the health of all concerned for you to move on.

If you do not know where to start to find a veterinarian, and your breeder is local to you, try your breeder's veterinarian first. By the time they have been breeding and raising dogs for a while, breeders have gained quite a lot of health care knowledge through experience and tend to be somewhat more demanding of veterinary care. If your breeder has have struck up a good relationship with a veterinarian, it is a good place for the new Shorthair owner to begin.

Select your Shorthair's veterinarian carefully. You will be much happier with a doctor whom you genuinely respect.

If you live far from your breeder or rescue adoption source, you may want to contact a breed club near you and phone a few Shorthair owners nearby and interview them about whom they use and why they like them. Ask what sorts of specific problems they have had with their dogs, and how the veterinarian helped them or put them at ease.

It is important for all of us to stay aware that veterinarians are not superhuman. They are medical professionals that probably started toward their profession because they had a special relationship with their own animals. We need to participate in our Shorthairs' health protocols and be vigilant about keeping informed, asking the right questions and challenging any decisions we think might compromise them. That is our job.

Work with Your Vet

Once you have the veterinarian you and your Shorthair feel comfortable with—one who really has the time for you and wants to answer your questions, work cooperatively with him. If you want to combine naturopathic approaches to preventive care with conventional veterinary treatment, you will need a veterinarian who is versed in both. If you are opposed to radical treatments, when more moderate ones might solve the problem, you owe it to yourself, your Shorthair and your veterinarian to let him know this before he takes your dog under his care.

Make Regular Appointments

Your Shorthair needs to have an annual medical exam. If necessary, your dog will receive booster shots of her vaccines. The annual exam is also a time for a weight check and a physical exam by a professional. Any active athletic dog, like a Shorthair, needs to be examined from time to time.

Vaccinations

Rabies

Rabies is a neurological virus that can be transmitted in the saliva of any warm-blooded animal. The virus migrates through the nervous system and back to the salivary glands. Once a dog has rabies, there is no cure. Rabies can be transmitted to

> **YOUR PUPPY'S VACCINES**
>
> Vaccines are given to prevent your dog from getting an infectious disease like canine distemper or rabies. Vaccines are the ultimate preventive medicine: they're given before your dog ever gets the disease so as to protect him from the disease. That's why it is necessary for your dog to be vaccinated routinely. Puppy vaccines start at eight weeks of age for the five-in-one DHLPP vaccine and are given every three to four weeks until the puppy is sixteen months old. Your veterinarian will put your puppy on a proper schedule and will remind you when to bring in your dog for shots.

humans through a bite or contact with infected saliva, and the cure for humans, if it is caught in time, is a series of painful shots.

Rabies prevention is a must, and you should discuss regular health checkups and a vaccination schedule with your veterinarian. Puppies should have their first rabies shots between 3 and 6 months of age, and at regular intervals thereafter. It is typical for the first rabies shot to provide protection for one year and all subsequent shots to protect for three years.

Immunization against rabies is critical. A puppy should receive her first rabies vaccine between 3 and 6 months of age.

PARVOVIRUS

Parvovirus is one of the greatest threats to a puppy or young dog. The severity of symptoms is unmatched by any other viral disease affecting your dog.

Full parvo immunization should be complete before you take your puppy out in public. Most breeders warn against taking a puppy home in a major city unless she is 3 months of age and has had full immunization, because parvovirus is such a serious problem in urban areas. Many people paper-train their pups in cities, so they will not have to go out of doors until they are fully immunized. This is particularly difficult with a Shorthair pup—a puppy from 8 to 12 weeks old needs a lot of exercise. If you plan to have a Shorthair in an urban environment, and are prepared to handle the exercise and energy needs of the breed, you may be better off leaving your puppy with the breeder until full immunizations are done.

OTHER VACCINATIONS

Vaccination is a prevention, not a cure. If a dog is already affected by an infectious disease, the vaccine will not help. Remember that a course of vaccines and a regular booster program for the first several years of life is important. Your breeder will have started the puppy shots at 5 and 8 weeks with inoculations for distemper, measles and parainfluenza vaccine (kennel cough). Distemper is highly contagious and most often strikes dogs 3 to 8 months of age. The dog will run a fever and appear to have a cold. Seek treatment from a veterinarian.

Internal Parasites

Dogs are subject to several types of worm infestations. Worms are quite common in sporting dogs, as they are often out in the field where wild animals that have parasites regularly leave their droppings. While you should not feel alarmed about this common problem, hygiene, flea control and regular testing will prevent a major problem. Have your Shorthair tested if she looks untidy or dull, or at any time she has diarrhea.

HEARTWORM

Heartworm is a life-threatening parasite borne by mosquitoes. It is impractical to try and control the mosquito population or to keep your Shorthair away from them, so prevention is important, if not critical. I give heartworm preventative every month of the year. Ask your veterinarian about the best prevention program for your dog.

INTESTINAL WORMS

There are several common kinds of worms to treat for in hunting dogs. Roundworms and whipworms can actually be transmitted from mother to puppy in utero or during nursing. It is common for breeders to treat for these worms starting between 2 and 3 weeks of age. Treatment should be repeated every two weeks until 3 months of age. Roundworms are not too serious if treated early, but they can be transmitted to humans, and children should be supervised when with dogs or in their surroundings. As most worm eggs are passed through feces, it is very important to have a diligent hygiene and pick up stool material daily and dispose of it.

External Parasites

TICKS AND FLEAS

Ticks have always been unwelcome guests, even before the horrors of Lyme disease. Ticks also carry Rocky Mountain Spotted Fever, babesiosis and ehrlichia. These are all tick-borne diseases, and while we once thought some of these diseases were confined to certain geographical areas in the U.S., we are discovering that they are reaching across the country. We have also learned that Lyme disease is carried by other kinds of ticks, in addition to the deer tick in the Northeast.

Protect your Shorthair from attracting ticks. Your dog will want to enjoy the great outdoors.

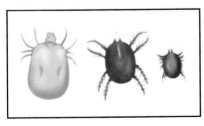

Three types of ticks (l-r): the wood tick, brown dog tick and deer tick.

Tick prevention is a tough problem with Shorthairs, particularly when they are often out in heavy cover, hunting or running for joy. The good news is that there are now a number of topical tick and flea controls recommended by most veterinarians that kill ticks before they ever bite the dog. Most of these also kill fleas. These have a long effective period, often up to a month for ticks and three months for fleas. Your veterinarian is the best source of more information on these products. Remember that these are pesticides, so use them only according to instructions.

While I am eager to prevent ticks from biting my Short-hairs, I have found the odd one here or there on the dogs when winter warms up unexpectedly, or if I have forgotten to use the preventative. If you find a tick on your dog, remove it with tweezers, making sure to get out the head and apply an antiseptic to the site.

Because Lyme vaccine is only designed for one tick-borne disease, and there are now three others for most regions to contend with, I give a routing autumn course of anti-biotic to all of my dogs. The nature of tick-borne diseases makes this treatment useful in the early stages of infec-tion. I have consulted with my veterinarian on this issue, and before you do this, you should consult with yours.

With the advent of the latest flea and tick treatments, my dogs have had no significant problem with either. If your Shorthair does get fleas, however, remember that the treatment will kill fleas, but that the pupal stage of a flea's life cycle is in a protective cocoon, not on your dog, but in your dog's environment. You may see some fleas around the house, even when you no longer see any on your Shorthair, as they will have hatched and be looking for their first meal. You may want to treat the environment to rid yourself of these remaining fleas, and treat again when any flea eggs are due to hatch. Consult with your veterinarian regarding the available products for this purpose, or call a professinal pest control service.

MITES

There are two major mite-related diseases that concern Shorthair owners: sarcoptic mange (scabies) and demo-dectic mange. Sarcoptic mange is caused by a spider-like mite that the dog picks up in the environment from contact with other dogs or other mammals that have it. It causes intense itching and extreme discomfort, so it is hard to miss that there is something wrong.

Demodex is a completely different problem. Some mites live everywhere in the environment causing no significant problems and demodex is normally one of these. When the Shorthair's immune system is compromised, however, the Demodectic mites thrive and multiply. You may note some spotty hair loss on the muzzle or crown of the head and on the extremities. If this occurs in the first year of life, the pup may simply be developing her own immune system as the immunities she has gotten from her dam are wearing off, and she needs to catch up. The veterinarian will usually prescribe an ointment to treat the affected areas, and the problem typically resolves. I usually try to support the dog's immune health with lots of exercise, outdoor play and immune-supportive nutrition. If you see large masses of demodex over large areas of the body of an older dog, it may be an indication of a severely compromised immune system. The prognosis may not be good.

Emergencies
INGESTED NON-FOOD ITEMS

Shorthairs carry things around in their mouths, chew seemingly incessantly and ingest a variety of things that are not food. A preventative rule is to Shorthair-proof the environment. Here are some of the things they may swallow, and how you can be alert and react.

Personal Possessions
Favorite among inappropriate items to ingest are nylon stockings or panty hose, socks or underwear. Of course, these are the things worn the closest to the owner's body, and carry the strongest scent. Sometimes socks will simply pass through the digestive tract. Stockings or panty hose may thread themselves quite a way through the bowel, and may even cut the bowel interior. If your Shorthair is straining, seems in pain or her bowel movement effort is unproductive, get her to a veterinarian or emergency facility.

Stones
On occasion you will find a Shorthair stone eater. Small stones seem to pass through the bowel without event.

Larger ones may obstruct the opening at the bowel end of the stomach and may have to be removed. The first sign is, once again, strained, unproductive attempts at bowel movement. This may be accompanied by attempts at vomiting. A radiograph (x-ray) will spot the blockage. Get to your veterinarian's office if your dog has a problem defecating.

Poisons

The most dangerous of the common household poisons is antifreeze. Keep it locked up, and make sure any spills or leaks are thoroughly scrubbed up. It is sweet to the taste, and dogs lick it up. If a dog ingests antifreeze in your presence, you can induce vomiting, and perhaps save her life. If you do not catch it at the time, the dog will almost surely die.

Some of the many household substances harmful to your dog.

Massive ingestion of chocolate, some poison plants, paint thinner, pesticides and all painkillers but plain or buffered aspirin are common household poisoning substances.

If you see your dog eat a poisonous substance, contact your veterinarian immediately and tell him that this is an emergency. If the dog is disoriented, drooling, convulsing, staggering, vomiting on her own, suffering fever, chills or is paralytic, she may have ingested a poison and you should immediately call your veterinarian.

PORCUPINES, RACCOONS AND SNAKES, OH NO!

Tangling with wildlife is a favorite fault of a Shorthair. After all, she is prey-driven, and most things look like prey to her. If she tangles with a porcupine, get her to the veterinarian for quill removal. Only if you are unable to get to a veterinarian should you attempt to remove quills yourself. If you must do this, get heavy shears or wire cutters and pliers. Steady and calm the dog. Cut off the ends of the quills, but leave enough quill that you can get a good grasp with the pliers, and pull them out. Apply topical antiseptic, and get to the veterinarian as soon as possible. The injuries are very painful and the risk of infection is substantial.

Raccoons, squirrels, opossums and other mammals can be rabies carriers. Keep some rubber gloves handy to handle the dog with should she have an encounter with a wild mammal. Get your dog to the veterinarian if stitches are needed and ask about a rabies booster shot.

Be prepared if your Shorthair's prey drive results in an unwanted encounter.

Some areas of the country do not have poisonous snakes. Some do. If you live in an area where snakes endanger your Shorthair, it is better to prepare than to repair. Snake-break your dog. Most of this is currently done with electronic collars designed to give the dog a harmless electrical shock when she approaches the dangerous object. The shock is strong enough to cause the dog to avoid what she associates with the pain—in this case, the snake. The device usually has several stimulation strengths and can be operated by remote control by the dog's handler.

If the dog just stumbles on a snake and is bitten, however, grab the dog, muzzle and immobilize her and get her to a veterinarian. Memorize what the snake looks like, or if it is dead, take it with you to the veterinarian. Your Shorthair's life may depend on identifying the snake.

Heatstroke and Exposure

Never leave your dog in a car in summer for any length of time unless the dog is crated in a cool wire crate with window or door ventilation. Even if you leave the windows open "a crack," the heat inside your car will mount to more than 100°F on a hot day in just a few minutes. In just thirty minutes, the heat will be enough to kill the dog. If the dog is secure in her crate, the windows can be left open, but you will be taking a chance of someone interfering with the dog. On very hot days, leave the dog home. She will be much happier, and she will be glad to see you when you get back.

When it is cold, a Shorthair needs to be moving around or her short coat will become her enemy. She cannot keep warm in a freezing situation unless she is under blankets, is wearing a dog coat or is very active. A cold car threatens serious exposure for Shorthairs; either be sure the bedding is thick and she has a dog coat, or leave her indoors during extreme cold.

On a hot summer's day, a car can become a dog's death trap. Leave your Shorthair home when temperatures rise.

Wounds

Shorthairs are somewhat like reckless kids on a holiday. They crash into things, leap over things and injure themselves. If your dog is hit by a vehicle, of course, you need to stop the bleeding, get a stretcher and get the dog to emergency care. In most other cases of injury, there are first aid treatments that you can employ. A tourniquet is useful for a deep cut to prevent blood loss while on the way to the veterinarian.

If the wound is a body wound, however, and not easily stanched by this treatment, you can apply pressure with the heal of your hand pressed over sterile gauze. Do not move the gauze if it becomes soaked, just add more.

Get the dog to professional care as soon as possible in all cases of serious wounds.

If the wound is minor, clean it with antiseptic to be sure it is free of debris, and treat it with either a powdered antiseptic/antibiotic, or one with a liquid base. It is never a bad idea to get a wound examined by a veterinarian. If your dog needs stitches, it is better to get them right away—after only a short period of time the edges of the wound begin to heal open, leaving the site ripe for infection.

In all field excursions, have a first aid kit at the ready, and note the veterinary office nearest to where you are hunting and exercising your Shorthair. Readiness and prevention are the watchwords for injury and accidents.

WHEN TO CALL THE VET

In any emergency situation, you should call your veterinarian immediately. You can make the difference in your dog's life by staying as calm as possible when you call and by giving the doctor or the assistant as much information as possible before you leave for the clinic. That way, the vet will be able to take immediate, specific action to remedy your dog's situation.

Emergencies include acute abdominal pain, suspected poisoning, snakebite, burns, frostbite, shock, dehydration, abnormal vomiting or bleeding, and deep wounds. You are the best judge of your dog's health, as you live with and observe her every day. Don't hesitate to call your veterinarian if you suspect trouble.

Licking

It is natural for a Shorthair to lick to clean herself, and licking a wound is also natural. If your Shorthair licks a wound or stitch site too much, she may remove stitches or open the wound. Cover the area with gauze bandage and disposable veterinary wrap, some adhesive tape and top it off with a spray or smear of some substance the dog cannot stand the taste of.

Lick Sores

If the dog develops a lick sore for no apparent reason, the real reason is very likely that she is bored, lacks sufficient exercise, is alone too much or is in an environment that makes her nervous or frightened. Naturally, the correct approach is to solve the cause. More exercise, more family time, more interesting things to do and a calmer family interaction will help prevent this in the future, but once it starts, it has to be healed up before the dog will stop licking the spot.

Spaying and Neutering

This topic is one of the most commonly discussed by veterinarians, dog owners and breeders. Given that, we would think the question would have already been resolved. Somehow, it is still under discussion.

It is my opinion that all dogs of either sex should be neutered before they reach hormonal maturity unless they are being held out as possible show dogs or as breeding prospects by an experienced breeder.

There are two primary reasons for having your dog spayed or neutered. The first is the health of the specific animal involved. Females have significantly less chance of developing mammary cancer later in life if they are spayed prior to first estrus or "heat" cycle. If you hunt your female Shorthair, you need not worry about her coming into season during hunting season and spoiling all your fun.

Quality time with the family will go far to maintain your Shorthair's health.

Neutered males display less dominance aggression, will not seek out females in season or act obsessively when there is a female in season around. One of the most important reasons to neuter your male Shorthair when he is young is the reduced risk of prostate cancer. Somehow, people resist neutering male Shorthairs more vigorously than they do spaying females. This sometimes takes on an almost tribal taboo. I have even had men tell me that male Shorthairs that are neutered do not hunt as well or do as well in field competition. That is simply not the case. A Shorthair's eagerness to hunt has to do with her blood, her nose, her prey drive and her brain, not her reproductive organs.

The second major reason that both male and female companion animals should be neutered is that they should not be bred. A purebred, AKC-registered dog is not necessarily a good candidate for breeding. Inexperienced people seldom consider the following:

Their beloved female dog may die carrying or whelping puppies or may develop a uterine infection called pyometra and die.

Whelping puppies is not always easy, and can be heartbreaking and expensive if something goes wrong. Leave it to the breeders. They are prepared for what may happen.

Finding qualified owners for Shorthairs is demanding and time-consuming. If the placement is not carefully done, the new owner may soon think twice about taking on a dog with such energy and enthusiasm. If a breeder is not prepared to take back any dog he has bred, for the life of the dog, she may end up in a shelter or pound and ultimately be put to sleep.

If you have aspirations of becoming a breeder, you should start by "apprenticing" to the best and most responsible breeder you can find and learn all of the pros and cons of taking on this responsibility before leaping into it. If you do less, you are not only threatening the health of your own beloved pet, you are threatening the health of the breed as a whole.

As Your Shorthair Ages

If you have followed all of the proper health protocols for a healthy Shorthair from nutrition to exercise to annual checkups with your veterinarian, there is no reason you should not enjoy your Shorthair to the fullest through all of her twelve to fourteen years. You may notice some slowing down around year twelve, and she may sleep more during the day than you have been used to, but she will be just as eager to awaken, eat and be with you as ever.

Sometimes Shorthairs weaken in the rear quarters at the very end, and some intervention with arthritis medication or naturopathic treatments can prolong a higher quality of life. Warts and some benign growths are natural in an aging dog and should not worry you unless they threaten the dog's well-being. Soon you will see silver threads among the liver on the muzzle and over the eyes. The look of the comedic, noble aristocrat will take on the look of the dignified senior diplomat.

You will want to feed a bit more carefully during this time of life, being sure that excess weight does not impact joints and muscles. Getting up and down stairs into late life depends on correct weight.

Slower walks in the sun will be your lot, and you will not have to worry about absorbing so much of that famous Shorthair energy. You will sit quietly with one another more often, watching television, reading or just being together quietly. Quiet hunting trips on easier grounds will still be fun for both of you, but be sure that your aging Shorthair can both hear you call and see who

An older Short-hair may slow down a bit and develop the dignified look of an elder statesman.

you are from a distance. Old age cataracts, which are perfectly normal in any dog, will make distance vision hazy.

This is the time of life when a comfy dog bed with soft foam fingers covered by plush fabric is right for your Shorthair. Placing the favorite bed in a sunny window in winter is wonderfully soothing to your sleeping friend.

It is time for the best memories, for appreciating what you have shared together, for spending quality time.

It may also be time to consider getting a new Shorthair. Sometimes oldsters can just be grumpy about a newbie on the block, but sometimes those aging muscles, bones and sinews are stimulated to stay in better shape because a strapping youngster is bounding about saying "Come On! Let's be Shorthairs." I encourage people to get a new pup before their old friend passes. It is part of staying happy.

When the time comes to say good-bye, we all hope we will wake one morning and our best friend will have just passed over to the Rainbow Bridge. This does not always happen, and we are often called upon to assist with this passing.

A senior dog is often taken with the energy of a young companion.

No person can tell another when it is time to relieve suffering, end pain and sustain dignity for the aged Shorthair. This must be a personal decision. Shorthairs, however, have full spirits and an uncanny way of letting their owners know just what to do. While most owners probably hold on too long for the sake of their own fear of loss, the Shorthair will tell you when it is time. You will know when you see it, even the first time. The bond of thousands of years of human/canine communication reaches an apex in this shared moment. Someone helped this puppy into the world, and assisted her with living happily in it. When it is time to relax life, it is only suitable that her master help her move on. At this time, all the friends you have come to know who belong to Shorthairs will support you and share. It is a fine community of common interest and mutual love of the breed.

Your Happy, Healthy Pet

Your Dog's Name _____

Name on Your Dog's Pedigree (if your dog has one) _____

_____

Where Your Dog Came From _____

_____

Your Dog's Birthday _____

Your Dog's Veterinarian

    Name   _____

    Address   _____

    Phone Number_____

    Emergency Number_____

Your Dog's Health

    Vaccines

    type _____ date given _____

    type _____ date given _____

    type _____ date given _____

    type _____ date given _____

    Heartworm

    date tested _____ type used_____ start date _____

Your Dog's License Number_____

Groomer's Name and Number _____

Dogsitter/Walker's Name and Number_____

Awards Your Dog Has Won

    Award _____ date earned _____

    Award _____ date earned _____

part three

Enjoying
your
Dog

Basic
Training

by Ian Dunbar, Ph.D., MRCVS

Training is the jewel in the crown—the most important aspect of doggy husbandry. There is no more important variable influencing dog behavior and temperament than the dog's education: A well-trained, well-behaved and good-natured puppydog is always a joy to live with, but an untrained and un-civilized dog can be a perpetual nightmare. Moreover, deny the dog an education and she will not have the opportunity to fulfill her own canine potential; neither will she have the ability to communicate effectively with her human companions.

Luckily, modern psychological training methods are easy, efficient, effective and, above all, considerably dog-friendly and user-friendly.

Doggy education is as simple as it is enjoyable. But before you can have a good time play-training with your new dog, you have to learn what to do and how to do it. There is no bigger variable influencing the success of dog training than the *owner's* experience and expertise. *Before you embark on the dog's education, you must first educate yourself.*

Basic Training for Owners

Ideally, basic owner training should begin well *before* you select your dog. Find out all you can about your chosen breed first, then master rudimentary training and handling skills. If you already have your puppydog, owner training is a dire emergency—the clock is ticking! Especially for puppies, the first few weeks at home are the most important and influential days in the dog's life. Indeed, the cause of most adolescent and adult problems may be traced back to the initial days the pup explores her new home. This is the time to establish the *status quo*—to teach the puppydog how you would like her to behave and so prevent otherwise quite predictable problems.

In addition to consulting breeders and breed books such as this one (which understandably have a positive breed bias), seek out as many pet owners with your breed as you can find. Good points are obvious. What you want to find out are the breed-specific *problems,* so you can nip them in the bud. In particular, you should talk to owners with *adolescent* dogs and make a list of all anticipated problems. Most important, *test drive* at least half a dozen adolescent and adult dogs of your breed yourself. An 8-week-old puppy is deceptively easy to handle, but she will acquire adult size, speed and strength in just four months, so you should learn now what to prepare for.

Puppy and pet dog training classes offer a convenient venue to locate pet owners and observe dogs in action. For a list of suitable trainers in your area, contact the Association of Pet Dog Trainers (see chapter 13). You may also begin your basic owner training by observing other owners in class. Watch as many classes and test drive as many dogs as possible. Select an upbeat, dog-friendly, people-friendly, fun-and-games, puppydog pet training class to learn the ropes. Also, watch training videos and read training books. You must find out what to do and how to do it *before* you have to do it.

Principles of Training

Most people think training comprises teaching the dog to do things such as sit, speak and roll over, but even a 4-week-old pup knows how to do these things already. Instead, the first step in training involves teaching the dog human words for each dog behavior and activity and for each aspect of the dog's environment. That way you, the owner, can more easily participate in the dog's domestic education by directing her to perform specific actions appropriately, that is, at the right time, in the right place and so on. Training opens communication channels, enabling an educated dog to at least understand her owner's requests.

In addition to teaching a dog *what* we want her to do, it is also necessary to teach her *why* she should do what we ask. Indeed, 95 percent of training revolves around motivating the dog *to want to do* what we want. Dogs often understand what their owners want; they just don't see the point of doing it—especially when the owner's repetitively boring and seemingly senseless instructions are totally at odds with much more pressing and exciting doggy distractions. It is not so much the dog that is being stubborn or dominant; rather, it is the owner who has failed to acknowledge the dog's needs and feelings and to approach training from the dog's point of view.

THE MEANING OF INSTRUCTIONS

The secret to successful training is learning how to use training lures to predict or prompt specific behaviors—to coax the dog to do what you want *when* you want. Any highly valued object (such as a treat or toy) may be used as a lure, which the dog will follow with her eyes and nose. Moving the lure in specific ways entices the dog to move her nose, head and entire body in specific ways. In fact, by learning the art of manipulating various lures, it is possible to teach the dog to assume virtually any body position and perform any action. Once you have control over the expression of the dog's behaviors and can elicit any body position or behavior at will, you can easily teach the dog to perform on request.

Teach your dog words for each activity she needs to know, like down.

Tell your dog what you want her to do, use a lure to entice her to respond correctly, then profusely praise and maybe reward her once she performs the desired action. For example, verbally request "Tina, sit!" while you move a squeaky toy upwards and backwards over the dog's muzzle (lure-movement and hand signal), smile knowingly as she looks up (to follow the lure) and sits down (as a result of canine anatomical engineering), then praise her to distraction ("Gooood Tina!"). Squeak the toy, offer a training treat and give your dog and yourself a pat on the back.

Being able to elicit desired responses over and over enables the owner to reward the dog over and over. Consequently, the dog begins to think training is fun. For example, the more the dog is rewarded for sitting, the more she enjoys sitting. Eventually the dog comes to realize that, whereas most sitting is appreciated, sitting immediately upon request usually prompts especially enthusiastic praise and a slew of high-level rewards. The dog begins to sit on cue much of the time, showing that she is starting to grasp the meaning of the owner's verbal request and hand signal.

WHY COMPLY?

Most dogs enjoy initial lure-reward training and are only too happy to comply with their owners' wishes. Unfortunately, repetitive drilling without appreciative feedback tends to diminish the dog's enthusiasm until she eventually fails to see the point of complying anymore. Moreover, as the dog approaches adolescence she becomes more easily distracted as she develops other interests. Lengthy sessions with repetitive exercises tend to bore and demotivate both parties. If it's not fun, the owner doesn't do it and neither does the dog.

Integrate training into your dog's life: The greater number of training sessions each day and the *shorter* they are, the more willingly compliant your dog will

To train your dog, you need gentle hands, a loving heart and a good attitude.

become. Make sure to have a short (just a few seconds) training interlude before every enjoyable canine activity. For example, ask your dog to sit to greet people, to sit before you throw her Frisbee and to sit for her supper. Really, sitting is no different from a canine "Please."

Also, include numerous short training interludes during every enjoyable canine pastime, for example, when playing with the dog or when she is running in the park. In this fashion, doggy distractions may be effectively converted into rewards for training. Just as all games have rules, fun becomes training . . . and training becomes fun.

Eventually, rewards actually become unnecessary to continue motivating your dog. If trained with consideration and kindness, performing the desired behaviors will become self-rewarding and, in a sense, your dog will motivate herself. Just as it is not necessary to reward a human companion during an enjoyable walk in the park, or following a game of tennis, it is hardly necessary to reward our best friend—the dog—for walking by our side or while playing fetch. Human company during enjoyable activities is reward enough for most dogs.

Even though your dog has become self-motivating, it's still good to praise and pet her a lot and offer rewards once in a while, especially for a good job well done. And if for no other reason, praising and rewarding others is good for the human heart.

Punishment

Without a doubt, lure-reward training is by far the best way to teach: Entice your dog to do what you want and then reward her for doing so. Unfortunately, a human shortcoming is to take the good for granted and to moan and groan at the bad. Specifically, the dog's many good behaviors are ignored while the owner focuses on punishing the dog for making mistakes. In extreme cases, instruction is *limited* to punishing mistakes made by a trainee dog, child, employee or husband, even though it has been proven punishment training is notoriously inefficient and ineffective and is decidedly unfriendly and combative. It teaches the dog that training is a drag, almost as quickly as it teaches the dog to dislike her trainer. Why treat our best friends like our worst enemies?

Punishment training is also much more laborious and time consuming. Whereas it takes only a finite amount of time to teach a dog what to chew, for example, it takes much, much longer to punish the dog for each and every mistake. Remember, *there is only one right way!* So why not teach that right way from the outset?!

To make matters worse, punishment training causes severe lapses in the dog's reliability. Since it is obviously impossible to punish the dog each and every time she misbehaves, the dog quickly learns to distinguish between those times when she must comply (so as to avoid impending punishment) and those times when she need not comply, because punishment is impossible. Such times include when the dog is off leash and 6 feet away, when the owner is otherwise engaged (talking to a friend, watching television, taking a shower, tending to the baby or chatting on the telephone) or when the dog is left at home alone.

Instances of misbehavior will be numerous when the owner is away, because even when the dog complied in the owner's looming presence, she did so unwillingly. The dog was forced to act against her will, rather than molding her will to want to please. Hence, when the owner is absent, not only does the dog know she need not comply, she simply does not want to. Again, the trainee is not a stubborn vindictive beast, but rather the trainer has failed to teach. Punishment training invariably creates unpredictable Jekyll and Hyde behavior.

Trainer's Tools

Many training books extol the virtues of a vast array of training paraphernalia and electronic and metallic gizmos, most of which are designed for canine restraint, correction and punishment, rather than for actual facilitation of doggy education. In reality, most effective training tools are not found in stores; they come from within ourselves. In addition to a willing dog, all you really need is a functional human brain, gentle hands, a loving heart and a good attitude.

In terms of equipment, all dogs do require a quality buckle collar to sport dog tags and to attach the leash (for safety and to comply with local leash laws). Hollow chew toys (like Kongs or sterilized longbones) and a dog bed or collapsible crate are musts for housetraining. Three additional tools are required:

1. specific lures (training treats and toys) to predict and prompt specific desired behaviors;

2. rewards (praise, affection, training treats and toys) to reinforce for the dog what a lot of fun it all is; and

3. knowledge—how to convert the dog's favorite activities and games (potential distractions to training) into "life-rewards," which may be employed to facilitate training.

The most powerful of these is *knowledge*. Education is the key! Watch training classes, participate in training classes, watch videos, read books, enjoy play-training with your dog and then your dog will say "Please," and your dog will say "Thank you!"

Housetraining

If dogs were left to their own devices, certainly they would chew, dig and bark for entertainment and then no doubt highlight a few areas of their living space with sprinkles of urine, in much the same way we decorate by hanging pictures. Consequently, when we ask a dog to live with us, we must teach her *where* she may dig, *where* she may perform her toilet duties, *what* she may chew and *when* she may bark. After all, when left at home alone for many hours, we cannot expect the dog to amuse herself by completing crosswords or watching the soaps on TV!

Also, it would be decidedly unfair to keep the house rules a secret from the dog, and then get angry and punish the poor critter for inevitably transgressing rules she did not even know existed. Remember: Without adequate education and guidance, the dog will be forced to establish her own rules—doggy rules—and most probably will be at odds with the owner's view of domestic living.

Since most problems develop during the first few days the dog is at home, prospective dog owners must be certain they are quite clear about the principles of housetraining *before* they get a dog. Early misbehaviors quickly become established as the *status quo*—

becoming firmly entrenched as hard-to-break bad habits, which set the precedent for years to come. Make sure to teach your dog good habits right from the start. Good habits are just as hard to break as bad ones!

Ideally, when a new dog comes home, try to arrange for someone to be present as much as possible during the first few days (for adult dogs) or weeks for puppies. With only a little forethought, it is surprisingly easy to find a puppy sitter, such as a retired person, who would be willing to eat from your refrigerator and watch your television while keeping an eye on the newcomer to encourage the dog to play with chew toys and to ensure she goes outside on a regular basis.

POTTY TRAINING

To teach the dog where to relieve herself:

1. never let her make a single mistake;
2. let her know where you want her to go; and
3. handsomely reward her for doing so: "GOOOOOOOD DOG!!!" liver treat, liver treat, liver treat!

Preventing Mistakes

A single mistake is a training disaster, since it heralds many more in future weeks. And each time the dog soils the house, this further reinforces the dog's unfortunate preference for an indoor, carpeted toilet. *Do not let an unhousetrained dog have full run of the house.*

When you are away from home, or cannot pay full attention, confine the dog to an area where elimination is appropriate, such as an outdoor run or, better still, a small, comfortable indoor kennel with access to an outdoor run. When confined in this manner, most dogs will naturally housetrain themselves.

If that's not possible, confine the dog to an area, such as a utility room, kitchen, basement or garage, where elimination may not be desired in the long run but as an interim measure it is certainly preferable to doing it all around the house. Use newspaper to cover the floor of the dog's day room. The newspaper may be used to soak up the urine and to wrap up and dispose of the feces. Once your dog develops a preferred spot for eliminating, it is only necessary to cover that part of the floor with newspaper. The smaller papered area may then be moved (only a little each day) towards the door to the outside. Thus the dog will develop the tendency to go to the door when she needs to relieve herself.

Never confine an unhousetrained dog to a crate for long periods. Doing so would force the dog to soil the crate and ruin its usefulness as an aid for housetraining (see the following discussion).

Teaching Where

In order to teach your dog where you would like her to do her business, you have to be there to direct the proceedings—an obvious, yet often neglected, fact of life. In order to be there to teach the dog *where* to go, you need to know *when* she needs to go. Indeed, the success of housetraining depends on the owner's ability to predict these times. Certainly, a regular feeding schedule will facilitate prediction somewhat, but there is nothing like "loading the deck" and influencing the timing of the outcome yourself!

The first few weeks at home are the most important and influential in your dog's life.

Whenever you are at home, make sure the dog is under constant supervision and/or confined to a small area. If already well trained, simply instruct the dog to lie down in her bed or basket. Alternatively, confine the dog to a crate (doggy den) or tie-down (a short, 18-inch lead that can be clipped to an eye hook in the baseboard near her bed). Short-term close confinement strongly inhibits urination and defecation, since the dog does not want to soil her sleeping area. Thus, when you release the puppydog each hour, she will definitely need to urinate immediately and defecate every third or fourth hour. Keep the dog confined to her doggy den and take her to her intended toilet area each hour, every hour and on the hour.

When taking your dog outside, instruct her to sit quietly before opening the door—she will soon learn to sit by the door when she needs to go out!

Teaching Why

Being able to predict when the dog needs to go enables the owner to be on the spot to praise and reward the dog. Each hour, hurry the dog to the intended toilet area in the yard, issue the appropriate instruction ("Go pee!" or "Go poop!"), then give the dog three to four minutes to produce. Praise and offer a couple of training treats when successful. The treats are important because many people fail to praise their dogs with feeling . . . and housetraining is hardly the time for understatement. So either loosen up and enthusiastically praise that dog: "Wuzzzer-wuzzer-wuzzer, hoooser good wuffer den? Hoooo went pee for Daddy?" Or say "Good dog!" as best you can and offer the treats for effect.

Following elimination is an ideal time for a spot of play-training in the yard or house. Also, an empty dog may be allowed greater freedom around the house for the next half hour or so, just as long as you keep an eye out to make sure she does not get into other kinds of mischief. If you are preoccupied and cannot pay full attention, confine the dog to her doggy den once more to enjoy a peaceful snooze or to play with her many chew toys.

If your dog does not eliminate within the allotted time outside—no biggie! Back to her doggy den, and then try again after another hour.

As I own large dogs, I always feel more relaxed walking an empty dog, knowing that I will not need to finish our stroll weighted down with bags of feces!

Beware of falling into the trap of walking the dog to get her to eliminate. The good ol' dog walk is such an enormous highlight in the dog's life that it represents the single biggest potential reward in domestic dogdom. However, when in a hurry, or during inclement weather, many owners abruptly terminate the walk the moment the dog has done her business. This, in effect, severely punishes the dog for doing the right thing, in the right place at the right time. Consequently, many dogs become strongly inhibited from eliminating outdoors because they know it will signal an abrupt end to an otherwise thoroughly enjoyable walk.

Instead, instruct the dog to relieve herself in the yard prior to going for a walk. If you follow the above instructions, most dogs soon learn to eliminate on cue. As soon as the dog eliminates, praise (and offer a treat or two)—"Good dog! Let's go walkies!" Use the walk as a reward for eliminating in the yard. If the dog does not go, put her back in her doggy den and think about a walk later on. You will find with a "No feces—no walk" policy, your dog will become one of the fastest defecators in the business.

If you do not have a backyard, instruct the dog to eliminate right outside your front door prior to the walk. Not only will this facilitate clean up and disposal of the feces in your own trash can but, also, the walk may again be used as a colossal reward.

CHEWING AND BARKING

Short-term close confinement also teaches the dog that occasional quiet moments are a reality of domestic living. Your puppydog is extremely impressionable during her first few weeks at home. Regular confinement at this time soon exerts a calming influence over the dog's personality. Remember, once the dog is housetrained and calmer, there will be a whole lifetime ahead for the dog to enjoy full run of the house and garden. On the other hand, by letting the newcomer have unrestricted access to the entire household and allowing her to run willy-nilly, she will most certainly develop a bunch of behavior problems in short order, no doubt necessitating confinement later in life. It would not be fair to remedially restrain and confine a dog you have trained, through neglect, to run free.

When confining the dog, make sure she always has an impressive array of suitable chew toys. Kongs and sterilized longbones (both readily available from pet stores) make the best chew toys, since they are hollow and may be stuffed with treats to heighten the dog's interest. For example, by stuffing the little hole at the top of a Kong with a small piece of freeze-dried liver, the dog will not want to leave it alone.

Remember, treats do not have to be junk food and they certainly should not represent extra calories. Rather, treats should be part of each dog's regular daily diet: Some food may be served in the dog's bowl for breakfast and dinner, some food may be used as training treats, and some food may be used for stuffing chew toys. I regularly stuff my dogs' many Kongs with different shaped biscuits and kibble.

Make sure your puppy has suitable chew toys.

The kibble seems to fall out fairly easily, as do the oval-shaped biscuits, thus rewarding the dog instantaneously for checking out the chew toys. The bone-shaped biscuits fall out after a while, rewarding the dog for worrying at the chew toy. But the triangular biscuits never come out. They remain inside the Kong as lures, maintaining the dog's fascination with her chew toy. To further focus the dog's interest, I always make sure to flavor the triangular biscuits by rubbing them with a little cheese or freeze-dried liver.

If stuffed chew toys are reserved especially for times the dog is confined, the puppydog will soon learn to enjoy quiet moments in her doggy den and she will quickly develop a chew-toy habit— a good habit! This is a simple *autoshaping* process; all the owner has to do is set up the situation and the dog all but trains herself— easy and effective. Even when the dog is given run of the house, her first inclination will be to indulge her rewarding chew-toy habit rather than destroy less-attractive household articles, such as curtains, carpets, chairs and compact disks. Similarly, a chew-toy chewer will be less inclined to scratch and chew herself excessively. Also, if the dog busies herself as a recreational chewer, she will be less inclined to develop into a recreational barker or digger when left at home alone.

Stuff a number of chew toys whenever the dog is left confined and remove the extra-special-tasting treats when you return. Your dog will now amuse herself with her chew toys before falling asleep and then resume playing with her chew toys when she expects you to return. Since most owner-absent misbehavior happens right after you leave and right before your expected return, your puppydog will now be conveniently preoccupied with her chew toys at these times.

Come and Sit

Most puppies will happily approach virtually anyone, whether called or not; that is, until they collide with adolescence and

To teach come, call your dog, open your arms as a welcoming signal, wave a toy or a treat and praise for every step in your direction.

develop other more important doggy interests, such as sniffing a multiplicity of exquisite odors on the grass. Your mission, Mr./Ms. Owner, is to teach and reward the pup for coming reliably, willingly and happily when called—and you have just three months to get it done. Unless adequately reinforced, your puppy's tendency to approach people will self-destruct by adolescence.

Call your dog ("Tina, come!"), open your arms (and maybe squat down) as a welcoming signal, waggle a treat or toy as a lure and reward the puppydog when she comes running. Do not wait to praise the dog until she reaches you—she may come 95 percent of the way and then run off after some distraction. Instead, praise the dog's *first* step towards you and continue praising enthusiastically for *every* step she takes in your direction.

When the rapidly approaching puppy dog is three lengths away from impact, instruct her to sit ("Tina, sit!") and hold the lure in front of you in an outstretched hand to prevent her from hitting you midchest and knocking you flat on your back! As Tina decelerates to nose the lure, move the treat upwards and backwards just over her muzzle with an upwards motion of your extended arm (palm-upwards). As the dog looks up to follow the lure, she will sit down (if she jumps up, you are holding the lure too high). Praise the dog for sitting. Move backwards and call her again. Repeat this many times over, always praising when Tina comes and sits; on occasion, reward her.

For the first couple of trials, use a training treat both as a lure to entice the dog to come and sit and as a reward for doing so. Thereafter, try to use different items as lures and rewards. For example, lure the dog with a Kong or Frisbee but reward her with a food treat. Or lure the dog with a food treat but pat her and throw a tennis ball as a reward. After just a few repetitions, dispense with the lures and rewards; the dog will begin to respond willingly to your verbal requests and hand signals just for the prospect of praise from your heart and affection from your hands.

Instruct every family member, friend and visitor how to get the dog to come and sit. Invite people over for a series of pooch parties; do not keep the pup a secret— let other people enjoy this puppy, and let the pup enjoy other people. Puppydog parties are not only fun, they easily attract a lot of people to help *you* train *your* dog. Unless you teach your dog how to meet people, that is, to sit for greetings, no doubt the dog will resort to jumping up. Then you and the visitors will get annoyed, and the dog will be punished. This is not fair. *Send out those invitations for puppy parties and teach your dog to be mannerly and socially acceptable.*

Even though your dog quickly masters obedient recalls in the house, her reliability may falter when playing in the backyard or local park. Ironically, it is *the owner* who has unintentionally trained the dog *not* to respond in these instances. By allowing the dog to play and run around and otherwise have a good time, but then to call the dog to put her on leash to take her home, the dog quickly learns playing is fun but training is a drag. Thus, playing in the park becomes a severe distraction, which works against training. Bad news!

Instead, whether playing with the dog off leash or on leash, request her to come at frequent intervals—say, every minute or so. On most occasions, praise and pet the dog for a few seconds while she is sitting, then tell her to go play again. For especially fast recalls, offer a couple of training treats and take the time to praise and pet the dog enthusiastically before releasing her. The dog will learn that coming when called is not necessarily the end of the play session, and neither is it the end of the world; rather, it signals an enjoyable, quality time-out with the owner before resuming play once more. In fact, playing in the park now becomes a very effective life-reward, which works to facilitate training by reinforcing each obedient and timely recall. Good news!

Sit, Down, Stand and Rollover

Teaching the dog a variety of body positions is easy for owner and dog, impressive for spectators and extremely useful for all. Using lure-reward techniques, it is possible to train several positions at once to verbal commands or hand signals (which impress the socks off onlookers).

Sit and *down*—the two control commands—prevent or resolve nearly a hundred behavior problems. For example, if the dog happily and obediently sits or lies down when requested, she cannot jump on visitors, dash out the front door, run around and chase her tail, pester other dogs, harass cats or annoy family, friends or strangers. Additionally, "Sit" or "Down" are the best emergency commands for off-leash control.

It is easier to teach and maintain a reliable sit than maintain a reliable recall. *Sit* is the purest and simplest of commands—either the dog is sitting or she is not. If there is any change of circumstances or potential danger in the park, for example, simply instruct the dog to sit. If she sits, you have a number of options: Allow the dog to resume playing when she is safe, walk up and put the dog on leash or call the dog. The dog will be much more likely to come when called if she has already acknowledged her compliance by sitting. If the dog does not sit in the park—train her to!

Stand and *rollover-stay* are the two positions for examining the dog. Your veterinarian will love you to distraction if you take a little time to teach the dog to stand still and roll over and play possum. Also, your vet bills will be smaller because it will take the veterinarian less time to examine your dog. The rollover-stay is an especially useful command and is really just a variation of the down-stay: Whereas the dog lies prone in the traditional down, she lies supine in the rollover-stay.

As with teaching come and sit, the training techniques to teach the dog to assume all other body positions on cue are user-friendly and dog-friendly. Simply give the appropriate request, lure the dog into the desired body position using a training treat or toy and then *praise* (and maybe reward) the dog as soon as she complies. Try not to touch the dog to get her to respond. If you teach the dog by guiding her into position, the dog will quickly learn that rump-pressure means sit, for example, but as yet you still have no control over your dog if she is just 6 feet away. It will still be necessary to teach the dog to sit on request. So do not make training a time-consuming two-step process; instead, teach the dog to sit to a verbal request or hand signal from the outset. Once the dog sits willingly when requested, by all means use your hands to pet the dog when she does so.

To teach **down** when the dog is already sitting, say "Tina, down!," hold the lure in one hand (palm down) and lower that hand to the floor between the dog's forepaws. As the dog lowers her head to follow the lure, slowly move the lure away from the dog just a fraction (in front of her paws). The dog will lie down as she stretches her nose forward to follow the lure. Praise the dog when she does so. If the dog stands up, you pulled the lure away too far and too quickly.

When teaching the dog to lie down from the standing position, say "Down" and lower the lure to the floor as before. Once the dog has lowered her forequarters and assumed a play bow, gently and slowly move the lure *towards* the dog between her forelegs. Praise the dog as soon as her rear end plops down.

After just a couple of trials it will be possible to alternate sits and downs and have the dog energetically perform doggy push-ups. Praise the dog a lot, and after half a dozen or so push-ups reward the dog with a training treat or toy. You will notice the more energetically you move your arm—upwards (palm up) to get the dog to sit, and downwards (palm down) to get the dog to lie down—the more energetically the dog responds to your requests. Now try training the dog in silence and you will notice she has also learned to respond to hand signals. Yeah! Not too shabby for the first session.

To teach **stand** from the sitting position, say "Tina, stand," slowly move the lure half a dog-length away from the dog's nose, keeping it at nose level, and praise the dog as she stands to follow the lure. As soon

Using a food lure to teach sit, down and stand. 1) "Phoenix, sit." 2) Hand palm upwards, move lure up and back over dog's muzzle. 3) "Good sit, Phoenix!" 4) "Phoenix, down." 5) Hand palm downwards, move lure down to lie between dog's forepaws. 6) "Phoenix, off. Good down, Phoenix!" 7) "Phoenix, sit!" 8) Palm upwards, move lure up and back, keeping it close to dog's muzzle. 9) "Good sit, Phoenix!"

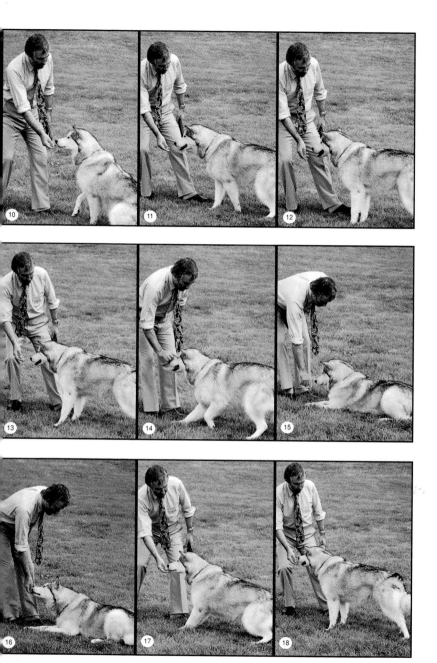

10) "Phoenix, stand!" 11) Move lure away from dog at nose height, then lower it a tad. 12) "Phoenix, off! Good stand, Phoenix!" 13) "Phoenix, down!" 14) Hand palm downwards, move lure down to lie between dog's forepaws. 15) "Phoenix, off! Good down-stay, Phoenix!" 16) "Phoenix, stand!" 17) Move lure away from dog's muzzle up to nose height. 18) "Phoenix, off! Good stand-stay, Phoenix. Now we'll make the vet and groomer happy!"

as the dog stands, lower the lure to just beneath the dog's chin to entice her to look down; otherwise she will stand and then sit immediately. To prompt the dog to stand from the down position, move the lure half a dog-length upwards and away from the dog, holding the lure at standing nose height from the floor.

Teaching *rollover* is best started from the down position, with the dog lying on one side, or at least with both hind legs stretched out on the same side. Say "Tina, bang!" and move the lure backwards and alongside the dog's muzzle to her elbow (on the side of her outstretched hind legs). Once the dog looks to the side and backwards, very slowly move the lure upwards to the dog's shoulder and backbone. Tickling the dog in the goolies (groin area) often invokes a reflex-raising of the hind leg as an appeasement gesture, which facilitates the tendency to roll over. If you move the lure too quickly and the dog jumps into the standing position, have patience and start again. As soon as the dog rolls onto her back, keep the lure stationary and mesmerize the dog with a relaxing tummy rub.

To teach *rollover-stay* when the dog is standing or moving, say "Tina, bang!" and give the appropriate hand signal (with index finger pointed and thumb cocked in true Sam Spade fashion), then in one fluid movement lure her to first lie down and then rollover-stay as above.

Teaching the dog to *stay* in each of the above four positions becomes a piece of cake after first teaching the dog not to worry at the toy or treat training lure. This is best accomplished by hand feeding dinner kibble. Hold a piece of kibble firmly in your hand and softly instruct "Off!" Ignore any licking and slobbering *for however long the dog worries at the treat*, but say "Take it!" and offer the kibble *the instant* the dog breaks contact with her muzzle. Repeat this a few times, and then up the ante and insist the dog remove her muzzle for one whole second before offering the kibble. Then progressively refine your criteria and have the dog not touch your hand (or treat) for longer and longer periods on each trial, such as for two seconds, four seconds, then six, ten, fifteen, twenty, thirty seconds and so on.

The dog soon learns: (1) worrying at the treat never gets results, whereas (2) noncontact is often rewarded after a variable time lapse.

Teaching *"Off!"* has many useful applications in its own right. Additionally, instructing the dog not to touch a training lure often produces spontaneous and magical stays. Request the dog to stand-stay, for example, and not to touch the lure. At first set your sights on a short two-second stay before rewarding the dog. (Remember, every long journey begins with a single step.) However, on subsequent trials, gradually and progressively increase the length of stay required to receive a reward. In no time at all your dog will stand calmly for a minute or so.

Relevancy Training

Once you have taught the dog what you expect her to do when requested to come, sit, lie down, stand, rollover and stay, the time is right to teach the dog *why* she should comply with your wishes. The secret is to have many (*many*) extremely short training interludes (two to five seconds each) at numerous (*numerous*) times during the course of the dog's day. Especially work with the dog immediately *before* the dog's good times and *during* the dog's good times. For example, ask your dog to sit and/or lie down each time before opening doors, serving meals, offering treats and tummy rubs; ask the dog to perform a few controlled doggy pushups before letting her off leash or throwing a tennis ball; and perhaps request the dog to sit-down-sit-stand-down-stand-rollover before inviting her to cuddle on the couch.

Similarly, request the dog to sit many times during play or on walks, and in no time at all the dog will be only too pleased to follow your instructions because she has learned that a compliant response heralds all sorts of goodies. Basically all you are trying to teach the dog is how to say please: "Please throw the tennis ball. Please may I snuggle on the couch."

Remember, it is important to keep training interludes short and to have many short sessions each and every day. The shortest (and most useful) session comprises asking the dog to sit and then go play during a play session. When trained this way, your dog will soon associate training with good times. In fact, the dog may be unable to distinguish between training and good times and, indeed, there should be no distinction. The warped concept that training involves forcing the dog to comply and/or dominating her will is totally at odds with the picture of a truly well-trained dog. In reality, enjoying a game of training with a dog is no different from enjoying a game of backgammon or tennis with a friend; and walking with a dog should be no different from strolling with a spouse, or with buddies on the golf course.

Walk by Your Side

Many people attempt to teach a dog to heel by putting her on a leash and physically correcting the dog when she makes mistakes. There are a number of things seriously wrong with this approach, the first being that most people do not want precision heeling; rather, they simply want the dog to follow or walk by their side. Second, when physically restrained during "training," even though the dog may grudgingly mope by your side when "handcuffed" on leash, let's see what happens when she is off leash. History! The dog is in the next county because she never enjoyed walking with you on leash and you have no control over her off leash. So let's just teach the dog off leash from the outset to *want* to walk with us. Third, if the dog has not been trained to heel, it is a trifle hasty to think about punishing the poor dog for making mistakes and breaking heeling rules she didn't even know existed. This is simply not fair! Surely, if the dog had been adequately taught how to heel, she would seldom make mistakes and hence there would be no need to correct the dog. Remember, each mistake and each correction (punishment) advertise the trainer's inadequacy, not the dog's. The dog is not stubborn, she is not stupid and she is not bad. Even if she were, she would still require training, so let's train her properly.

Let's teach the dog to *enjoy* following us and to *want* to walk by our side off leash. Then it will be easier to teach high-precision off-leash heeling patterns if desired. Before going on outdoor walks, it is necessary to teach the dog not to pull. Then it becomes easy to teach on-leash walking and heeling because the dog already wants to walk with you, she is familiar with the desired walking and heeling positions and she knows not to pull.

FOLLOWING

Start by training your dog to follow you. Many puppies will follow if you simply walk away from them and maybe click your fingers or chuckle. Adult dogs may require additional enticement to stimulate them to follow, such as a training lure or, at the very least, a lively trainer. To teach the dog to follow: (1) keep walking and (2) walk away from the dog. If the dog attempts to lead or lag, change pace; slow down if the dog forges too far ahead, but speed up if she lags too far behind. Say "Steady!" or "Easy!" each time before you slow down and "Quickly!" or "Hustle!" each time before you speed up, and the dog will learn to change pace on cue. If the dog lags or leads too far, or if she wanders right or left, simply walk quickly in the opposite direction and maybe even run away from the dog and hide.

Practicing is a lot of fun; you can set up a course in your home, yard or park to do this. Indoors, entice the dog to follow upstairs, into a bedroom, into the bathroom, downstairs, around the living room couch, zigzagging between dining room chairs and into the kitchen for dinner. Outdoors, get the dog to follow around park benches, trees, shrubs and along walkways and lines in the grass. (For safety outdoors, it is advisable to attach a long line on the dog, but never exert corrective tension on the line.)

Remember, following has a lot to do with attitude—*your* attitude! Most probably your dog will *not* want to follow Mr. Grumpy Troll with the personality of wilted lettuce. Lighten up—walk with a jaunty step, whistle a happy tune, sing, skip and tell jokes to your dog and she will be right there by your side.

BY YOUR SIDE

It is smart to train the dog to walk close on one side or the other—either side will do, your choice. When walking, jogging or cycling, it is generally bad news to have the dog suddenly cut in front of you. In fact, I train my dogs to walk "By my side" and "Other side"—both very useful instructions. It is possible to position the dog fairly accurately by looking to the appropriate side and clicking your fingers or slapping your thigh on that side. A precise positioning may be attained by holding a training lure, such as a chew toy, tennis ball or food treat. Stop and stand still several times throughout the walk, just as you would when window shopping or meeting a friend. Use the lure to make sure the dog slows down and stays close whenever you stop.

When teaching the dog to heel, we generally want her to sit in heel position when we stop. Teach heel

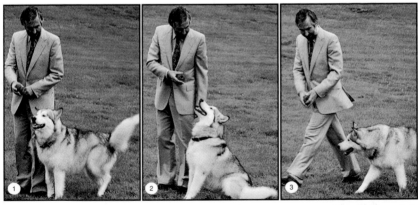

Using a toy to teach sit-heel-sit sequences: 1) "Phoenix, sit!" Standing still, move lure up and back over dog's muzzle . . . 2) to position dog sitting in heel position on your left side. 3) Say "Phoenix, heel!" and walk ahead, wagging lure in left hand. Change lure to right hand in preparation for sit signal. Say "Sit" and then . . .

position at the standstill and the dog will learn that the default heel position is sitting by your side (left or right—your choice, unless you wish to compete in obedience trials, in which case the dog must heel on the left).

Several times a day, stand up and call your dog to come and sit in heel position—"Tina, heel!" For example, instruct the dog to come to heel each time there are commercials on TV, or each time you turn a page of a novel, and the dog will get it in a single evening.

Practice straight-line heeling and turns separately. With the dog sitting at heel, teach her to turn in place. After each quarter-turn, half-turn or full turn in place, lure the dog to sit at heel. Now it's time for short straight-line heeling sequences, no more than a few steps at a time. Always think of heeling in terms of sit-heel-sit sequences—start and end with the dog in position and do your best to keep her there when moving. Progressively increase the number of steps in each sequence. When the dog remains close for 20 yards of straight-line heeling, it is time to add a few turns and then sign up for a happy-heeling obedience class to get some advice from the experts.

4) use hand signal to lure dog to sit as you stop. Eventually, dog will sit automatically at heel whenever you stop. 5) "Good dog!"

No Pulling on Leash

You can start teaching your dog not to pull on leash anywhere—in front of the television or outdoors—but regardless of location, you must not take a single step with tension in the leash. For a reason known only to dogs, even just a couple of paces of pulling on leash is intrinsically motivating and diabolically rewarding. Instead, attach the leash to the dog's collar, grasp the other end firmly with both hands held close to your chest, and stand still—do not budge an inch. Have somebody watch you with a stopwatch to time your progress, or else you will never believe this will work and so you will not even try the exercise, and your shoulder and the dog's neck will be traumatized for years to come.

Stand still and wait for the dog to stop pulling, and to sit and/or lie down. All dogs stop pulling and sit eventually. Most take only a couple of minutes; the all-time record is 22½ minutes. Time how long it takes. Gently praise the dog when she stops pulling, and as soon as she sits, enthusiastically praise the dog and take just one step forward, then immediately stand still. This single step usually demonstrates the ballistic reinforcing nature of pulling on leash; most dogs explode to the end of the leash, so be prepared for the strain. Stand firm and wait for the dog to sit again. Repeat this half a dozen times and you will probably notice a progressive reduction in the force of the dog's one-step explosions and a radical reduction in the time it takes for the dog to sit each time.

As the dog learns "Sit we go" and "Pull we stop," she will begin to walk forward calmly with each single step and automatically sit when you stop. Now try two steps before you stop. Wooooooo! Scary! When the dog has mastered two steps at a time, try for three. After each success, progressively increase the number of steps in the sequence: try four steps and then six, eight, ten and twenty steps before stopping. Congratulations! You are now walking the dog on leash.

Whenever walking with the dog (off leash or on leash), make sure you stop periodically to practice a few position commands and stays before instructing the dog to "Walk on!" (Remember, you want the dog to be compliant everywhere, not just in the kitchen when her dinner is at hand.) For example, stopping every 25 yards to briefly train the dog amounts to over 200 training interludes within a single 3-mile stroll. And each training session is in a different location. You will not believe the improvement within just the first mile of the first walk.

To put it another way, integrating training into a walk offers 200 separate opportunities to use the continuance of the walk as a reward to reinforce the dog's education. Moreover, some training interludes may comprise continuing education for the dog's walking skills: Alternate short periods of the dog walking calmly by your side with periods when the dog is allowed to sniff and investigate the environment. Now sniffing odors on the grass and meeting other dogs become rewards which reinforce the dog's calm and mannerly demeanor. Good Lord! Whatever next? Many enjoyable walks together of course. Happy trails!

THE IMPORTANCE OF TRICKS

Nothing will improve a dog's quality of life better than having a few tricks under her belt. Teaching any trick expands the dog's vocabulary, which facilitates communication and improves the owner's control. Also, specific tricks help prevent and resolve specific behavior problems. For example, by teaching the dog to fetch her toys, the dog learns carrying a toy makes the owner happy and, therefore, will be more likely to chew her toy than other inappropriate items.

More important, teaching tricks prompts owners to lighten up and train with a sunny disposition. Really, tricks should be no different from any other behaviors we put on cue. But they are. When teaching tricks, owners have a much sweeter attitude, which in turn motivates the dog and improves her willingness to comply. The dog feels tricks are a blast, but formal commands are a drag. In fact, tricks are so enjoyable, they may be used as rewards in training by asking the dog to come, sit and down-stay and then rollover for a tummy rub. Go on, try it: Crack a smile and even giggle when the dog promptly and willingly lies down and stays.

Most important, performing tricks prompts onlookers to smile and giggle. Many people are scared of dogs, especially large ones. And nothing can be more off-putting for a dog than to be constantly confronted by strangers who don't like her because of her size or the way she looks. Uneasy people put the dog on edge, causing her to back off and bark, only frightening people all the more. And so a vicious circle develops, with the people's fear fueling the dog's fear *and vice versa*. Instead, tie a pink ribbon to your dog's collar and practice all sorts of tricks on walks and in the park, and you will be pleasantly amazed how it changes people's attitudes toward your friendly dog. The dog's repertoire of tricks is limited only by the trainer's imagination. Below I have described three of my favorites:

SPEAK AND SHUSH

The training sequence involved in teaching a dog to bark on request is no different from that used when training any behavior on cue: request—lure—response—reward. As always, the secret of success lies in finding an effective lure. If the dog always barks at the doorbell, for example, say "Rover, speak!", have an accomplice ring the doorbell, then reward the dog for barking. After a few woofs, ask Rover to "Shush!", waggle a food treat under her nose (to entice her to sniff and thus to shush), praise her when quiet and eventually offer the treat as a reward. Alternate "Speak" and "Shush," progressively increasing the length of shush-time between each barking bout.

PLAY BOW

With the dog standing, say "Bow!" and lower the food lure (palm upwards) to rest between the dog's forepaws. Praise as the dog lowers her forequarters and sternum to the ground (as when teaching the down), but then lure the dog to stand and offer the treat. On successive trials, gradually increase the length of time the dog is required to remain in the play bow posture in order to gain a food reward. If the dog's rear end collapses into a down, say nothing and offer no reward; simply start over.

BE A BEAR

With the dog sitting backed into a corner to prevent her from toppling over backwards, say "Be a bear!" With bent paw and palm down, raise a lure upwards and backwards along the top of the dog's muzzle. Praise the dog when she sits up on her haunches and offer the treat as a reward. To prevent the dog from standing on her hind legs, keep the lure closer to the dog's muzzle. On each trial, progressively increase the length of time the dog is required to sit up to receive a food reward. Since lure-reward training is so easy, teach the dog to stand and walk on her hind legs as well!

Teaching "Be a Bear"

chapter 9

Getting

Active

with your Dog

by Bardi McLennan

Once you and your dog have graduated from basic obedience training and are beginning to work together as a team, you can take part in the growing world of dog activities. There are so many fun things to do with your dog! Just remember, people and dogs don't always learn at the same pace, so don't be upset if you (or your dog) need more than two basic training courses before your team becomes operational. Even smart dogs don't go straight to college from kindergarten!

Just as there are events geared to certain types of dogs, so there are ones that are more appealing to certain types of people. In some

128

activities, you give the commands and your dog does the work (upland game hunting is one example), while in others, such as agility, you'll both get a workout. You may want to aim for prestigious titles to add to your dog's name, or you may want nothing more than the sheer enjoyment of being around other people and their dogs. Passive or active, participation has its own rewards.

Consider your dog's physical capabilities when looking into any of the canine activities. It's easy to see that a Basset Hound is not built for the racetrack, nor would a Chihuahua be the breed of choice for pulling a sled. A loyal dog will attempt almost anything you ask him to do, so it is up to you to know your dog's limitations. A dog must be physically sound in order to compete at any level in athletic activities, and being mentally sound is a definite plus. Advanced age, however, may not be a deterrent. Many dogs still hunt and herd at ten or twelve years of age. It's entirely possible for dogs to be "fit at 50." Take your dog for a checkup, explain to your vet the type of activity you have in mind and be guided by his or her findings.

All dogs seem to love playing flyball.

You needn't be restricted to breed-specific sports if it's only fun you're after. Certain AKC activities are limited to designated breeds; however, as each new trial, test or sport has grown in popularity, so has the variety of breeds encouraged to participate at a fun level.

But don't shortchange your fun, or that of your dog, by thinking only of the basic function of her breed. Once a dog has learned how to learn, she can be taught to do just about anything as long as the size of the dog is right for the job and you both think it is fun and rewarding. In other words, you are a team.

To get involved in any of the activities detailed in this chapter, look for the names and addresses of the organizations that sponsor them in Chapter 13. You can also ask your breeder or a local dog trainer for contacts.

You can compete in obedience trials with a well trained dog.

Official American Kennel Club Activities

The following tests and trials are some of the events sanctioned by the AKC and sponsored by various dog clubs. Your dog's expertise will be rewarded with impressive titles. You can participate just for fun, or be competitive and go for those awards.

OBEDIENCE

Training classes begin with pups as young as three months of age in kindergarten puppy training, then advance to pre-novice (all exercises on lead) and go on to novice, which is where you'll start off-lead work. In obedience classes dogs learn to sit, stay, heel and come through a variety of exercises. Once you've got the basics down, you can enter obedience trials and work toward earning your dog's first degree, a C.D. (Companion Dog).

The next level is called "Open," in which jumps and retrieves perk up the dog's interest. Passing grades in competition at this level earn a C.D.X. (Companion Dog Excellent). Beyond that lies the goal of the most ambitious—Utility (U.D. and even U.D.X. or OTCh, an Obedience Champion).

AGILITY

All dogs can participate in the latest canine sport to have gained worldwide popularity for its fun and excitement, agility. It began in England as a canine version of horse show-jumping, but because dogs are more agile and able to perform on verbal commands, extra feats were added such as climbing, balancing and racing through tunnels or in and out of weave poles. Many of the obstacles (regulation or homemade) can be set up in your own backyard. If the agility bug bites, you could end up in international competition!

For starters, your dog should be obedience trained, even though, in the beginning, the lessons may all be taught on lead. Once the dog understands the commands (and you do, too), it's as easy as guiding the dog over a prescribed course, one obstacle at a time. In competition, the race is against the clock, so wear your running shoes! The dog starts with 200 points and the judge deducts for infractions and misadventures along the way.

All dogs seem to love agility and respond to it as if they were being turned loose in a playground paradise. Your dog's enthusiasm will be contagious; agility turns into great fun for dog and owner.

FIELD TRIALS AND HUNTING TESTS

There are field trials and hunting tests for the sporting breeds—retrievers, spaniels and pointing breeds, and for some hounds—Bassets, Beagles and Dachshunds. Field trials are competitive events that test a dog's ability to perform the functions for which she was bred. Hunting tests, which are open to retrievers,

---

TITLES AWARDED BY THE AKC

Conformation: Ch. (Champion)

Obedience: CD (Companion Dog); CDX (Companion Dog Excellent); UD (Utility Dog); UDX (Utility Dog Excellent); OTCh. (Obedience Trial Champion)

Field: JH (Junior Hunter); SH (Senior Hunter); MH (Master Hunter); AFCh. (Amateur Field Champion); FCh. (Field Champion)

Lure Coursing: JC (Junior Courser); SC (Senior Courser)

Herding: HT (Herding Tested); PT (Pre-Trial Tested); HS (Herding Started); HI (Herding Intermediate); HX (Herding Excellent); HCh. (Herding Champion)

Tracking: TD (Tracking Dog); TDX (Tracking Dog Excellent)

Agility: NAD (Novice Agility); OAD (Open Agility); ADX (Agility Excellent); MAX (Master Agility)

Earthdog Tests: JE (Junior Earthdog); SE (Senior Earthdog); ME (Master Earthdog)

Canine Good Citizen: CGC

Combination: DC (Dual Champion—Ch. and Fch.); TC (Triple Champion—Ch., Fch., and OTCh.)

---

spaniels and pointing breeds only, are noncompetitive and are a means of judging the dog's ability as well as that of the handler.

Hunting is a very large and complex part of canine sports, and if you own one of the breeds that hunts, the events are a great treat for your dog and you. He gets to do what he was bred for, and you get to work with him and watch him do it. You'll be proud of and amazed at what your dog can do.

Fortunately, the AKC publishes a series of booklets on these events, which outline the rules and regulations and include a glossary of the sometimes complicated terms. The AKC also publishes newsletters for field trialers and hunting test enthusiasts. The United Kennel Club (UKC) also has informative materials for the hunter and his dog.

Retrievers and other sporting breeds get to do what they're bred to in hunting tests.

HERDING TESTS AND TRIALS

Herding, like hunting, dates back to the first known uses man made of dogs. The interest in herding today is widespread, and if you own a herding breed, you can join in the activity. Herding dogs are tested for their natural skills to keep a flock of ducks, sheep or cattle together. If your dog shows potential, you can start at the testing level, where your dog can earn a title for showing an inherent herding ability. With training you can advance to the trial level, where your dog should be capable of controlling even difficult livestock in diverse situations.

LURE COURSING

The AKC Tests and Trials for Lure Coursing are open to traditional sighthounds—Greyhounds, Whippets,

Borzoi, Salukis, Afghan Hounds, Ibizan Hounds and Scottish Deerhounds—as well as to Basenjis and Rhodesian Ridgebacks. Hounds are judged on overall ability, follow, speed, agility and endurance. This is possibly the most exciting of the trials for spectators, because the speed and agility of the dogs is awesome to watch as they chase the lure (or "course") in heats of two or three dogs at a time.

TRACKING

Tracking is another activity in which almost any dog can compete because every dog that sniffs the ground when taken outdoors is, in fact, tracking. The hard part comes when the rules as to what, when and where the dog tracks are determined by a person, not the dog! Tracking tests cover a large area of fields, woods and roads. The tracks are laid hours before the dogs go to work on them, and include "tricks" like cross-tracks and sharp turns. If you're interested in search-and-rescue work, this is the place to start.

This tracking dog is hot on the trail.

EARTHDOG TESTS FOR SMALL TERRIERS AND DACHSHUNDS

These tests are open to Australian, Bedlington, Border, Cairn, Dandie Dinmont, Smooth and Wire Fox, Lakeland, Norfolk, Norwich, Scottish, Sealyham, Skye, Welsh and West Highland White Terriers as well as Dachshunds. The dogs need no prior training for this terrier sport. There is a qualifying test on the day of the event, so dog and handler learn the rules on the spot. These tests, or "digs," sometimes end with informal races in the late afternoon.

Here are some of the extracurricular obedience and racing activities that are not regulated by the AKC or UKC, but are generally run by clubs or a group of dog fanciers and are often open to all.

Canine Freestyle This activity is something new on the scene and is variously likened to dancing, dressage or ice skating. It is meant to show the athleticism of the dog, but also requires showmanship on the part of the dog's handler. If you and your dog like to ham it up for friends, you might want to look into freestyle.

Lure coursing lets sighthounds do what they do best—run!

Scent Hurdle Racing Scent hurdle racing is purely a fun activity sponsored by obedience clubs with members forming competing teams. The height of the hurdles is based on the size of the shortest dog on the team. On a signal, one team dog is released on each of two side-by-side courses and must clear every hurdle before picking up its own dumbbell from a platform and returning over the jumps to the handler. As each dog returns, the next on that team is sent. Of course, that is what the dogs are supposed to do. When the dogs improvise (going under or around the hurdles, stealing another dog's dumbbell, and so forth), it no doubt frustrates the handlers, but just adds to the fun for everyone else.

Flyball This type of racing is similar, but after negotiating the four hurdles, the dog comes to a flyball box, steps on a lever that releases a tennis ball into the air, catches the ball and returns over the hurdles to the starting point. This game also becomes extremely fun for spectators because the dogs sometimes cheat by catching a ball released by the dog in the next lane. Three titles can be earned—Flyball Dog (F.D.), Flyball Dog Excellent (F.D.X.) and Flyball Dog Champion (Fb.D.Ch.)—all awarded by the North American Flyball Association, Inc.

Dogsledding The name conjures up the Rocky Mountains or the frigid North, but you can find dogsled clubs in such unlikely spots as Maryland, North Carolina and Virginia! Dogsledding is primarily for the Nordic breeds such as the Alaskan Malamutes, Siberian Huskies and Samoyeds, but other breeds can try. There are some practical backyard applications to this sport, too. With parental supervision, almost any strong dog could pull a child's sled.

Coming over the A-frame on an agility course.

These are just some of the many recreational ways you can get to know and understand your multifaceted dog better and have fun doing it.

Your Dog
and your
Family

by Bardi McLennan

Adding a dog automatically increases your family by one, no matter whether you live alone in an apartment or are part of a mother, father and six kids household. The single-person family is fair game for numerous and varied canine misconceptions as to who is dog and who pays the bills, whereas a dog in a houseful of children will consider himself to be just one of the gang, littermates all. One dog and one child may give a dog reason to believe they are both kids or both dogs. Either interpretation requires parental supervision and sometimes speedy intervention.

As soon as one paw goes through the door into your home, Rufus (or Rufina) has to make many adjustments to become a part of your family. Your job is to make him fit in as painlessly as possible. An older dog may have some frame of reference from past experience, but to a 10-week-old puppy, everything is brand new: people, furniture, stairs, when and where people eat, sleep or watch TV, his own place and everyone else's space, smells, sounds, outdoors—everything!

Puppies, and newly acquired dogs of any age, do not need what we think of as "freedom." If you leave a new dog or puppy loose in the house, you will almost certainly return to chaotic destruction and the dog will forever after equate your homecoming with a time of punishment to be dreaded. It is unfair to give your dog what amounts to "freedom to get into trouble." Instead, confine him to a crate for brief periods of your absence (up to three or four hours) and, for the long haul, a workday for example, confine him to one untrashable area with his own toys, a bowl of water and a radio left on (low) in another room.

Lots of pets get along with each other just fine.

For the first few days, when not confined, put Rufus on a long leash tied to your wrist or waist. This umbilical cord method enables the dog to learn all about you from your body language and voice, and to learn by his own actions which things in the house are NO! and which ones are rewarded by "Good dog." House-training will be easier with the pup always by your side. Speaking of which, accidents do happen. That goal of "completely housetrained" takes up to a year, or the length of time it takes the pup to mature.

The All-Adult Family

Most dogs in an adults-only household today are likely to be latchkey pets, with no one home all day but the

dog. When you return after a tough day on the job, the
dog can and should be your relaxation therapy. But
going home can instead be a daily frustration.

Separation anxiety is a very common problem for the
dog in a working household. It may begin with whines
and barks of loneliness, but it will soon escalate into a
frenzied destruction derby. That is why it is so important to set aside the time to teach a dog to relax when
left alone in his confined area and to understand that
he can trust you to return.

Let the dog get used to your work schedule in easy
stages. Confine him to one room and go in and out of
that room over and over again. Be casual about it. No
physical, voice or eye contact. When the pup no longer
even notices your comings and goings, leave the house
for varying lengths of time, returning to stay home for
a few minutes and gradually increasing the time away.
This training can take days, but the dog is learning that
you haven't left him forever and that he can trust you.

Any time you leave the dog, but especially during this
training period, be casual about your departure. No
anxiety-building fond farewells. Just "Bye" and go!
Remember the "Good dog" when you return to find
everything more or less as you left it.

If things are a mess (or even a disaster) when you
return, greet the dog, take him outside to eliminate,
and then put him in his crate while you clean up. Rant
and rave in the shower! *Do not* punish the dog. You
were not there when it happened, and the rule is: Only
punish as you catch the dog in the act of wrongdoing.
Obviously, it makes sense to get your latchkey puppy
when you'll have a week or two to spend on these training essentials.

Family weekend activities should include Rufus whenever possible. Depending on the pup's age, now is the
time for a long walk in the park, playtime in the backyard, a hike in the woods. Socializing is as important as
health care, good food and physical exercise, so visiting Aunt Emma or Uncle Harry and the next-door

neighbor's dog or cat is essential to developing an out-going, friendly temperament in your pet.

If you are a single adult, socializing Rufus at home and away will prevent him from becoming overly protective of you (or just overly attached) and will also prevent such behavioral problems as dominance or fear of strangers.

Babies

Whether already here or on the way, babies figure larger than life in the eyes of a dog. If the dog is there first, let him in on all your baby preparations in the house. When baby arrives, let Rufus sniff any item of clothing that has been on the baby before Junior comes home. Then let Mom greet the dog first before introducing the new family member. Hold the baby down for the dog to see and sniff, but make sure some-one's holding the dog on lead in case of any sudden moves. Don't play keep-away or tease the dog with the baby, which only invites undesirable jump-ing up.

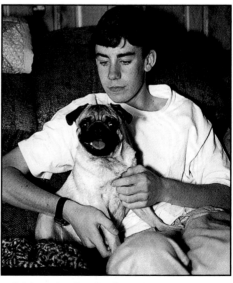

The dog and the baby are "family," and for starters can be treated almost as equals. Things rapidly change, however, espe-cially when baby takes to creeping around on all fours on the dog's turf or, better yet, has yummy pudding all over her face and hands! That's when a lot of things in the dog's and baby's lives become more separate than equal.

Dogs are perfect confidants.

Toddlers make terrible dog owners, but if you can't avoid the combination, use patient discipline (that is, positive teaching rather than punishment), and use time-outs before you run out of patience.

A dog and a baby (or toddler, or an assertive young child) should never be left alone together. Take the dog with you or confine him. With a baby or youngsters in the house, you'll have plenty of use for that wonderful canine safety device called a crate!

Young Children

Any dog in a house with kids will behave pretty much as the kids do, good or bad. But even good dogs and good children can get into trouble when play becomes rowdy and active.

Legs bobbing up and down, shrill voices screeching, a ball hurtling overhead, all add up to exuberant frustration for a dog who's just trying to be part of the gang. In a pack of puppies, any legs or toys being chased would be caught by a set of teeth, and all the pups involved would understand that is how the game is played. Kids do not understand this, nor do parents tolerate it. Bring Rufus indoors before you have reason to regret it. This is time-out, not a punishment.

Teach children how to play nicely with a puppy.

You can explain the situation to the children and tell them they must play quieter games until the puppy learns not to grab them with his mouth. Unfortunately, you can't explain it that easily to the dog. With adult supervision, they will learn how to play together.

Young children love to tease. Sticking their faces or wiggling their hands or fingers in the dog's face is teasing. To another person it might be just annoying, but it is threatening to a dog. There's another difference: We can make the child stop by an explanation, but the only way a dog can stop it is with a warning growl and then with teeth. Teasing is the major cause of children being bitten by their pets. Treat it seriously.

140

Older Children

The best age for a child to get a first dog is between the ages of 8 and 12. That's when kids are able to accept some real responsibility for their pet. Even so, take the child's vow of "I will never *ever* forget to feed (brush, walk, etc.) the dog" for what it's worth: a child's good intention at that moment. Most kids today have extra lessons, soccer practice, Little League, ballet, and so forth piled on top of school schedules. There will be many times when Mom will have to come to the dog's rescue. "I walked the dog for you so you can set the table for me" is one way to get around a missed appointment without laying on blame or guilt.

Kids in this age group make excellent obedience trainers because they are into the teaching/learning process themselves and they lack the self-consciousness of adults. Attending a dog show is something the whole family can enjoy, and watching Junior Showmanship may catch the eye of the kids. Older children can begin to get involved in many of the recreational activities that were reviewed in the previous chapter. Some of the agility obstacles, for example, can be set up in the backyard as a family project (with an adult making sure all the equipment is safe and secure for the dog).

Older kids are also beginning to look to the future, and may envision themselves as veterinarians or trainers or show dog handlers or writers of the next Lassie best-seller. Dogs are perfect confidants for these dreams. They won't tell a soul.

Other Pets

Introduce all pets tactfully. In a dog/cat situation, hold the dog, not the cat. Let two dogs meet on neutral turf—a stroll in the park or a walk down the street—with both on loose leads to permit all the normal canine ways of saying hello, including routine sniffing, circling, more sniffing, and so on. Small creatures such as hamsters, chinchillas or mice must be kept safe from their natural predators (dogs and cats).

Festive Family Occasions

Parties are great for people, but not necessarily for puppies. Until all the guests have arrived, put the dog in his crate or in a room where he won't be disturbed. A socialized dog can join the fun later as long as he's not underfoot, annoying guests or into the hors d'oeuvres.

There are a few dangers to consider, too. Doors opening and closing can allow a puppy to slip out unnoticed in the confusion, and you'll be organizing a search party instead of playing host or hostess. Party food and buffet service are not for dogs. Let Rufus party in his crate with a nice big dog biscuit.

At Christmas time, not only are tree decorations dangerous and breakable (and perhaps family heirlooms), but extreme caution should be taken with the lights, cords and outlets for the tree lights and any other festive lighting. Occasionally a dog lifts a leg, ignoring the fact that the tree is indoors. To avoid this, use a canine repellent, made for gardens, on the tree. Or keep him out of the tree room unless supervised. And whatever you do, *don't* invite trouble by hanging his toys on the tree!

Car Travel

Before you plan a vacation by car or RV with Rufus, be sure he enjoys car travel. Nothing spoils a holiday quicker than a carsick dog! Work within the dog's comfort level. Get in the car with the dog in his crate or attached to a canine car safety belt and just sit there until he relaxes. That's all. Next time, get in the car, turn on the engine and go nowhere. Just sit. When that is okay, turn on the engine and go around the block. Now you can go for a ride and include a stop where you get out, leaving the dog for a minute or two.

On a warm day, always park in the shade and leave windows open several inches. And return quickly. It only takes 10 minutes for a car to become an overheated steel death trap.

Motel or Pet Motel?

Not all motels or hotels accept pets, but you have a much better choice today than even a few years ago. To find a dog-friendly lodging, look at *On the Road Again With Man's Best Friend*, a series of directories that detail bed and breakfasts, inns, family resorts and other hotels/motels. Some places require a refundable deposit to cover any damage incurred by the dog. More B&Bs accept pets now, but some restrict the size.

If taking Rufus with you is not feasible, check out boarding kennels in your area. Your veterinarian may offer this service, or recommend a kennel or two he or she is familiar with. Go see the facilities for yourself, ask about exercise, diet, housing, and so on. Or, if you'd rather have Rufus stay home, look into bonded petsitters, many of whom will also bring in the mail and water your plants.

Your Dog
and your
Community

by Bardi McLennan

Step outside your home with your dog and you are no longer just family, you are both part of your community. This is when the phrase "responsible pet ownership" takes on serious implications. For starters, it means you pick up after your dog—not just occasionally, but every time your dog eliminates away from home. That means you have joined the Plastic Baggy Brigade! You always have plastic sandwich bags in your pocket and several in the car. It means you teach your kids how to use them, too. If you think this is "yucky," just imagine what

the person (a non-doggy person) who inadvertently steps in the mess thinks!

Your responsibility extends to your neighbors: To their ears (no annoying barking); to their property (their garbage, their lawn, their flower beds, their cat—especially their cat); to their kids (on bikes, at play); to their kids' toys and sports equipment.

There are numerous dog-related laws, ranging from simple dog licensing and leash laws to those holding you liable for any physical injury or property damage done by your dog. These laws are in place to protect everyone in the community, including you and your dog. There are town ordinances and state laws which are by no means the same in all towns or all states. Ignorance of the law won't get you off the hook. The time to find out what the laws are where you live is now.

Be sure your dog's license is current. This is not just a good local ordinance, it can make the difference between finding your lost dog or not. Many states now require proof of rabies vaccination and that the dog has been spayed or neutered before issuing a license. At the same time, keep up the dog's annual immunizations.

Dressing your dog up makes him appealing to strangers.

Never let your dog run loose in the neighborhood. This will not only keep you on the right side of the leash law, it's the outdoor version of the rule about not giving your dog "freedom to get into trouble."

Good Canine Citizen

Sometimes it's hard for a dog's owner to assess whether or not the dog is sufficiently socialized to be accepted by the community at large. Does Rufus or Rufina display good, controlled behavior in public? The AKC's Canine Good Citizen program is available through many dog organizations. If your dog passes the test, the title "CGC" is earned.

The overall purpose is to turn your dog into a good neighbor and to teach you about your responsibility to your community as a dog owner. Here are the ten things your dog must do willingly:

1. Accept a stranger stopping to chat with you.
2. Sit and be petted by a stranger.
3. Allow a stranger to handle him or her as a groomer or veterinarian would.
4. Walk nicely on a loose lead.
5. Walk calmly through a crowd.
6. Sit and down on command, then stay in a sit or down position while you walk away.
7. Come when called.
8. Casually greet another dog.
9. React confidently to distractions.
10. Accept being left alone with someone other than you and not become overly agitated or nervous.

Schools and Dogs

Schools are getting involved with pet ownership on an educational level. It has been proven that children who are kind to animals are humane in their attitude toward other people as adults.

A dog is a child's best friend, and so children are often primary pet owners, if not the primary caregivers. Unfortunately, they are also the ones most often bitten by dogs. This occurs due to a lack of understanding that pets, no matter how sweet, cuddly and loving, are still animals. Schools, along with parents, dog clubs, dog fanciers and the AKC, are working to change all that with video programs for children not only in grade school, but in the nursery school and pre-kindergarten age group. Teaching youngsters how to be responsible dog owners is important community work. When your dog has a CGC, volunteer to take part in an educational classroom event put on by your dog club.

Boy Scout Merit Badge

A Merit Badge for Dog Care can be earned by any Boy Scout ages 11 to 18. The requirements are not easy, but amount to a complete course in responsible dog care and general ownership. Here are just a few of the things a Scout must do to earn that badge:

> Point out ten parts of the dog using the correct names.

> Give a report (signed by parent or guardian) on your care of the dog (feeding, food used, housing, exercising, grooming and bathing), plus what has been done to keep the dog healthy.

> Explain the right way to obedience train a dog, and demonstrate three comments.

> Several of the requirements have to do with health care, including first aid, handling a hurt dog, and the dangers of home treatment for a serious ailment.

> The final requirement is to know the local laws and ordinances involving dogs.

There are similar programs for Girl Scouts and 4-H members.

Local Clubs

Local dog clubs are no longer in existence just to put on a yearly dog show. Today, they are apt to be the hub of the community's involvement with pets. Dog clubs conduct educational forums with big-name speakers, stage demonstrations of canine talent in a busy mall and take dogs of various breeds to schools for class-room discussion.

The quickest way to feel accepted as a member in a club is to volunteer your services! Offer to help with something—anything—and watch your popularity (and your interest) grow.

Therapy Dogs

Once your dog has earned that essential CGC and reliably demonstrates a steady, calm temperament, you could look into what therapy dogs are doing in your area.

Therapy dogs go with their owners to visit patients at hospitals or nursing homes, generally remaining on leash but able to coax a pat from a stiffened hand, a smile from a blank face, a few words from sealed lips or a hug from someone in need of love.

Nursing homes cover a wide range of patient care. Some specialize in care of the elderly, some in the treatment of specific illnesses, some in physical therapy. Children's facilities also welcome visits from trained therapy dogs for boosting morale in their pediatric patients. Hospice care for the terminally ill and the at-home care of AIDS patients are other areas

Your dog can make a difference in lots of lives.

where this canine visiting is desperately needed. Therapy dog training comes first.

There is a lot more involved than just taking your nice friendly pooch to someone's bedside. Doing therapy dog work involves your own emotional stability as well as that of your dog. But once you have met all the requirements for this work, making the rounds once a week or once a month with your therapy dog is possibly the most rewarding of all community activities.

Disaster Aid

This community service is definitely not for everyone, partly because it is time-consuming. The initial training is rigorous, and there can be no let-up in the continuing workouts, because members are on call 24 hours a day to go wherever they are needed at a moment's notice. But if you think you would like to be able to assist in a disaster, look into search-and-rescue work. The network of search-and-rescue volunteers is worldwide, and all members of the American Rescue Dog Association (ARDA) who are qualified to do this work are volunteers who train and maintain their own dogs.

Physical Aid

Most people are familiar with Seeing Eye dogs, which serve as blind people's eyes, but not with all the other work that dogs are trained to do to assist the disabled. Dogs are also specially trained to pull wheelchairs, carry school books, pick up dropped objects, open and close doors. Some also are ears for the deaf. All these assistance-trained dogs, by the way, are allowed anywhere "No Pet" signs exist (as are therapy dogs when

Making the rounds with your therapy dog can be very rewarding.

properly identified). Getting started in any of this fascinating work requires a background in dog training and canine behavior, but there are also volunteer jobs ranging from answering the phone to cleaning out kennels to providing a foster home for a puppy. You have only to ask.

part four

Beyond the Basics

Recommended Reading

Books

ABOUT HEALTH CARE

Ackerman, Lowell. *Guide to Skin and Haircoat Problems in Dogs.* Loveland, Colo.: Alpine Publications, 1994.

Alderton, David. *The Dog Care Manual.* Hauppauge, N.Y.: Barron's Educational Series, Inc., 1986.

American Kennel Club. *American Kennel Club Dog Care and Training.* New York: Howell Book House, 1991.

Bamberger, Michelle, DVM. *Help! The Quick Guide to First Aid for Your Dog.* New York: Howell Book House, 1995.

Carlson, Delbert, DVM, and James Giffin, MD. *Dog Owner's Home Veterinary Handbook.* New York: Howell Book House, 1992.

DeBitetto, James, DVM, and Sarah Hodgson. *You & Your Puppy.* New York: Howell Book House, 1995.

Humphries, Jim, DVM. *Dr. Jim's Animal Clinic for Dogs.* New York: Howell Book House, 1994.

McGinnis, Terri. *The Well Dog Book.* New York: Random House, 1991.

Pitcairn, Richard and Susan. *Natural Health for Dogs.* Emmaus, Pa.: Rodale Press, 1982.

ABOUT DOG SHOWS

Hall, Lynn. *Dog Showing for Beginners.* New York: Howell Book House, 1994.

Nichols, Virginia Tuck. *How to Show Your Own Dog.* Neptune, N. J.: TFH, 1970.

Vanacore, Connie. *Dog Showing, An Owner's Guide.* New York: Howell Book House, 1990.

ABOUT TRAINING

Ammen, Amy. *Training in No Time*. New York: Howell Book House, 1995.

Baer, Ted. *Communicating With Your Dog*. Hauppauge, N.Y.: Barron's Educational Series, Inc., 1989.

Benjamin, Carol Lea. *Dog Problems*. New York: Howell Book House, 1989.

Benjamin, Carol Lea. *Dog Training for Kids*. New York: Howell Book House, 1988.

Benjamin, Carol Lea. *Mother Knows Best*. New York: Howell Book House, 1985.

Benjamin, Carol Lea. *Surviving Your Dog's Adolescence*. New York: Howell Book House, 1993.

Bohnenkamp, Gwen. *Manners for the Modern Dog*. San Francisco: Perfect Paws, 1990.

Dibra, Bashkim. *Dog Training by Bash*. New York: Dell, 1992.

Dunbar, Ian, PhD, MRCVS. *Dr. Dunbar's Good Little Dog Book*, James & Kenneth Publishers, 2140 Shattuck Ave. #2406, Berkeley, Calif. 94704. (510) 658–8588. Order from the publisher.

Dunbar, Ian, PhD, MRCVS. *How to Teach a New Dog Old Tricks*, James & Kenneth Publishers. Order from the publisher; address above.

Dunbar, Ian, PhD, MRCVS, and Gwen Bohnenkamp. Booklets on *Preventing Aggression; Housetraining; Chewing; Digging; Barking; Socialization; Fearfulness; and Fighting*, James & Kenneth Publishers. Order from the publisher; address above.

Evans, Job Michael. *People, Pooches and Problems*. New York: Howell Book House, 1991.

Kilcommons, Brian and Sarah Wilson. *Good Owners, Great Dogs*. New York: Warner Books, 1992.

McMains, Joel M. *Dog Logic—Companion Obedience*. New York: Howell Book House, 1992.

Rutherford, Clarice and David H. Neil, MRCVS. *How to Raise a Puppy You Can Live With*. Loveland, Colo.: Alpine Publications, 1982.

Volhard, Jack and Melissa Bartlett. *What All Good Dogs Should Know: The Sensible Way to Train*. New York: Howell Book House, 1991.

ABOUT BREEDING

Harris, Beth J. Finder. *Breeding a Litter, The Complete Book of Prenatal and Postnatal Care*. New York: Howell Book House, 1983.

Holst, Phyllis, DVM. *Canine Reproduction*. Loveland, Colo.: Alpine Publications, 1985.

Walkowicz, Chris and Bonnie Wilcox, DVM. *Successful Dog Breeding, The Complete Handbook of Canine Midwifery.* New York: Howell Book House, 1994.

ABOUT ACTIVITIES

American Rescue Dog Association. *Search and Rescue Dogs.* New York: Howell Book House, 1991.

Barwig, Susan and Stewart Hilliard. *Schutzhund.* New York: Howell Book House, 1991.

Beaman, Arthur S. *Lure Coursing.* New York: Howell Book House, 1994.

Daniels, Julie. *Enjoying Dog Agility—From Backyard to Competition.* New York: Doral Publishing, 1990.

Davis, Kathy Diamond. *Therapy Dogs.* New York: Howell Book House, 1992.

Gallup, Davis Anne. *Running With Man's Best Friend.* Loveland, Colo.: Alpine Publications, 1986.

Habgood, Dawn and Robert. *On the Road Again With Man's Best Friend.* New England, Mid-Atlantic, West Coast and Southeast editions. Selective guides to area bed and breakfasts, inns, hotels and resorts that welcome guests and their dogs. New York: Howell Book House, 1995.

Holland, Vergil S. *Herding Dogs.* New York: Howell Book House, 1994.

LaBelle, Charlene G. *Backpacking With Your Dog.* Loveland, Colo.: Alpine Publications, 1993.

Simmons-Moake, Jane. *Agility Training, The Fun Sport for All Dogs.* New York: Howell Book House, 1991.

Spencer, James B. *Hup! Training Flushing Spaniels the American Way.* New York: Howell Book House, 1992.

Spencer, James B. *Point! Training the All-Seasons Birddog.* New York: Howell Book House, 1995.

Tarrant, Bill. *Training the Hunting Retriever.* New York: Howell Book House, 1991.

Volhard, Jack and Wendy. *The Canine Good Citizen.* New York: Howell Book House, 1994.

General Titles

Haggerty, Captain Arthur J. *How to Get Your Pet Into Show Business.* New York: Howell Book House, 1994.

McLennan, Bardi. *Dogs and Kids, Parenting Tips.* New York: Howell Book House, 1993.

Moran, Patti J. *Pet Sitting for Profit, A Complete Manual for Professional Success.* New York: Howell Book House, 1992.

Scalisi, Danny and Libby Moses. *When Rover Just Won't Do, Over 2,000 Suggestions for Naming Your Dog.* New York: Howell Book House, 1993.

Sife, Wallace, PhD. *The Loss of a Pet.* New York: Howell Book House, 1993.

Wrede, Barbara J. *Civilizing Your Puppy.* Hauppauge, N.Y.: Barron's Educational Series, 1992.

Magazines

The AKC GAZETTE, The Official Journal for the Sport of Purebred Dogs. American Kennel Club, 51 Madison Ave., New York, NY.

Bloodlines Journal. United Kennel Club, 100 E. Kilgore Rd., Kalamazoo, MI.

Dog Fancy. Fancy Publications, 3 Burroughs, Irvine, CA 92718

Dog World. Maclean Hunter Publishing Corp., 29 N. Wacker Dr., Chicago, IL 60606.

Videos

"SIRIUS Puppy Training," by Ian Dunbar, PhD, MRCVS. James & Kenneth Publishers, 2140 Shattuck Ave. #2406, Berkeley, CA 94704. Order from the publisher.

"Training the Companion Dog," from Dr. Dunbar's British TV Series, James & Kenneth Publishers. (See address above).

The American Kennel Club produces videos on every breed of dog, as well as on hunting tests, field trials and other areas of interest to purebred dog owners. For more information, write to AKC/Video Fulfillment, 5580 Centerview Dr., Suite 200, Raleigh, NC 27606.

Resources

Breed Clubs

Every breed recognized by the American Kennel Club has a national (parent) club. National clubs are a great source of information on your breed. You can get the name of the secretary of the club by contacting:

The American Kennel Club
51 Madison Avenue
New York, NY 10010
(212) 696-8200

There are also numerous all-breed, individual breed, obedience, hunting and other special-interest dog clubs across the country. The American Kennel Club can provide you with a geographical list of clubs to find ones in your area. Contact them at the above address.

Registry Organizations

Registry organizations register purebred dogs. The American Kennel Club is the oldest and largest in this country, and currently recognizes over 130 breeds. The United Kennel Club registers some breeds the AKC doesn't (including the American Pit Bull Terrier and the Miniature Fox Terrier) as well as many of the same breeds. The others included here are for your reference; the AKC can provide you with a list of foreign registries.

American Kennel Club
51 Madison Avenue
New York, NY 10010

United Kennel Club (UKC)
100 E. Kilgore Road
Kalamazoo, MI 49001-5598

American Dog Breeders Assn.
P.O. Box 1771
Salt Lake City, UT 84110
(Registers American Pit Bull Terriers)

Canadian Kennel Club
89 Skyway Avenue
Etobicoke, Ontario
Canada M9W 6R4

National Stock Dog Registry
P.O. Box 402
Butler, IN 46721
(Registers working stock dogs)

Orthopedic Foundation for Animals (OFA)
2300 E. Nifong Blvd.
Columbia, MO 65201-3856
(Hip registry)

Activity Clubs

Write to these organizations for information on the
activities they sponsor.

American Kennel Club
51 Madison Avenue
New York, NY 10010
(Conformation Shows, Obedience Trials, Field
Trials and Hunting Tests, Agility, Canine Good

Citizen, Lure Coursing, Herding, Tracking,
Earthdog Tests, Coonhunting.)

United Kennel Club
100 E. Kilgore Road
Kalamazoo, MI 49001-5598
(Conformation Shows, Obedience Trials, Agility,
Hunting for Various Breeds, Terrier Trials and
more.)

North American Flyball Assn.
1342 Jeff St.
Ypsilanti, MI 48198

International Sled Dog Racing Assn.
P.O. Box 446
Norman, ID 83848-0446

North American Working Dog Assn., Inc.
Southeast Kreisgruppe
P.O. Box 833
Brunswick, GA 31521

Trainers

Association of Pet Dog Trainers
P.O. Box 385
Davis, CA 95617
(800) PET–DOGS

American Dog Trainers' Network
161 West 4th St.
New York, NY 10014
(212) 727–7257

**National Association of Dog Obedience
Instructors**
2286 East Steel Rd.
St. Johns, MI 48879

Associations

American Dog Owners Assn.
1654 Columbia Tpk.
Castleton, NY 12033
(Combats anti-dog legislation)

Delta Society
P.O. Box 1080
Renton, WA 98057-1080
(Promotes the human/animal bond through
pet-assisted therapy and other programs)

Dog Writers Assn. of America (DWAA)
Sally Cooper, Secy.
222 Woodchuck Ln.
Harwinton, CT 06791

National Assn. for Search and Rescue (NASAR)
P.O. Box 3709
Fairfax, VA 22038

Therapy Dogs International
6 Hilltop Road
Mendham, NJ 07945